R AND E RESEARCH ASSOCIATES
4843 Mission Street, San Francisco 94112
18581 McFarland Avenue, Saratoga, California 95070

Publishers and Distributors of Ethnic Studies
Editor: Adam S. Eterovich
Publisher: Robert D. Reed

Library of Congress Card Catalog Number

73-82389

ISBN

0-88247-228-3

TABLE OF CONTENTS

PREFACE v

I   The Beginning of Anti Japanese Sentiment: "The Japs Must Go!"--
1890-1905. 1

II   The Asiatic Exclusion League: Its Formation, Agitation, and
Expansion--1905-1909 11

III   The Stormy Petrel of Labor Circles: The League and Politics--
1905-1913. 26

IV   The Origins of the Alien Land Law: Facts and Myths. 51

V   The Politics of Nativism--1907-1912. 65

VI   The Alien Land Law of 1913: Grape Juice Diplomacy and a Bit
of Political Buncombe. 83

Appendix A--Senate Bill 1074 by Senator Thomas Finn 98

Appendix B--The Alien Land Law of 1913, proposed by the Asiatic
           Exclusion League. 100

Appendix C--The Alien Land Law of 1913, Chapter 113, <u>Statutes of
           California</u>, 1913. 102

Appendix D--The Alien Land Law of 1920, "Measures Submitted to
           Electors," <u>Statutes of California</u>, 1921 104

Appendix E--The Alien Land Law of 1923, Chapter 441,
           <u>Statues of California</u>, 1923 108

BIBLIOGRAPHY. 112

PREFACE

Information for this thesis was first gathered in History 101 in 1962. Exposure to books and articles along with many encouraging suggestions from Professor Joseph A. McGowan, led me to investigate the origins of the Alien Land Law of 1913.

Especial thanks must be given to the librarians in the California Room at the State Library who were extremely friendly, patient, and helpful while I gathered more than 5,000 notes from three newspapers covering a twenty year period. The Sacramento State College inter-library loan service was helpful in obtaining thesis and dissertations from the Bancroft Library in Berkeley and the very cooperative library at Stanford University.

Dr. W. N. Davis's course in State and Federal Archives opened a whole new vista of source material and provided primary documents on important individuals and organizations.

It hardly seems possible that this thesis could ever have been written without the encouragement, friendliness, and moral persuasiveness of Joseph A. McGowan.

Last, but by far not least, my wife, Joyce, has earned my devoted thanks. With the patience of Job and the faith of Penelope, she provided much of the inspiration and motivation to see the job through.

CHAPTER I

THE BEGINNING OF ANTI-JAPANESE SENTIMENT: "THE JAPS MUST GO!"
1890-1905

Mr. Rindge. Well, I think there is a good many things at the bottom of it. In the first place, the Japanese, on account of their enterprise and their ability and their desire to work--personally I am a great admirer of the race; they are a people who, I take it, bear the torch. There is nothing in the way of labor trouble with them. They go right ahead with their work and they can stand the climate down there [in the delta], and one of the reasons for the agitation is that ever since the time Dennis Carney--[sic].
Mr. Siegel. (interposing) Just who is Dennis Carney?
Mr. Rindge. The Chinese exclusion. It has been a kind of political proposition. Well, it has been a paradise for politicians, raising their cries against Orientals.

Sworn testimony of Fred H. Rindge, Sacramento, July 16, 1920, before House Immigration and Naturalization Committee, Japanese Immigration Hearings, p. 460.

CHAPTER I

THE BEGINNING OF ANTI-JAPANESE SENTIMENT: "THE JAPS MUST GO!"
1890-1905

The origins of Japanese nativism during the 1890's should be seen to some extent as an extension of the Chinese exclusion movement since it was at this time that newspapers, politicians and labor leaders began building an anti-Japanese stereotype. Such politicians and labor leaders as San Francisco's mayor, James D. Phelan,[1] Congressman Everis A. Hayes,[2] Denis Kearney and Walter Macarthur[3]--all active in Chinese exclusion--tended to apply the same philosophy to the Japanese.

Denis Kearney, perhaps best known for his sandlot oratory against the Chinese during the mid-1870's, had taken to speaking on a dry-goods box at 4th and K streets in Sacramento by 1892. Stating that it was his twenty-ninth speech in two years against the Japanese (the first to be given outside the city of San Francisco), Kearney typified the Japanese as being without Christian virtues since they are

---

[1] Before the election of November 1920, the senior Senator, James D. Phelan, was flooding the state "with statements showing that the Senator made a speech 35 years ago against Chinese immigration." San Francisco Chronicle, September 28, 1920, p. 4/2. Many of Phelan's anti-Chinese speeches will be found in the Chinese Pamphlets, California Room, Sacramento State Library.

[2] San Francisco Call, February 5, 1906, p. 13/4. A member of the House of Representatives from California's 5th district and a member of the Asiatic Exclusion League, Hayes kept the League well represented and informed on Congressional immigration bills. At one Exclusion meeting, Hayes commented: "If I had my way, I would not only exclude the Asiatics, but I would pack up all the Japs and Chinese in this country and send them back where they belong (applause)," Asiatic Exclusion League, Proceeding, May 10, 1908, p. 10; hereafter cited as A. E. L., Proceedings. For other articles which illustrate Hayes' connection to the League and his desire to extend the provision of the Chinese Immigration Act to the Japanese, see the San Francisco Call, October 26, 1908, p. 1/1; San Francisco Call, April 8, 1909, p. 7/3; San Francisco Call, December 15, 1912, p. 1/3; cf. also his speeches in the House of Representatives on January 23, 1907 and February 25, 1909.

[3] Mary Roberts Coolidge, Chinese Immigration, p. 244. Macarthur spoke frequently at Japanese exclusion meetings and was a member of the executive committee of the Asiatic Exclusion League. Cf. San Francisco Call, January 10, 1906, p. 7/1; January 14, 1906, p. 52/3; December 24, 1906, p. 1/4; May 13, 1907, p. 7/3. As United States shipping commissioner in San Francisco, Macarthur did not hesitate to state his position on the Japanese in California. "Nature and time has proved again and again that there can be no mingling of two distinct race types without serious injury to the progress of both. There must always be a master to keep the other race subdued. That is the whole trouble with the Japanese in California; they are trying to assert their superiority over the Caucasians." San Francisco Call, April 30, 1913, p. 45. Cf. also, W. Macarthur, "Review of Exclusion History," in Annals of the American Academy of Political and Social Science, LXXXXIII (January 1921), pp. 38-42.

as "free to mingle together [in Japan] as are the beasts of the field."⁴ He complained that Japanese, so numerous in California, will "demoralize and disorganize" the labor market, while being educated in American schools at public expense.

> We are paying out money for the purpose of allowing fully developed men who know no morals but vice to sit beside our sons and our daughters in our public schools that they may help to debauch., demoralize and teach them the vices which are the customs of the country whence they came. These Japs work for almost nothing for the sake of getting an education .... As Democrats and Republicans, it becomes our duty to make our leaders take up and put in their platforms a plank demanding Congress to pass a Japanese exclusion law.⁵

A little over a month before, on May 30, Kearney had given a rousing speech in San Francisco, claiming that the Pacific Mail, Northern Pacific, Canadian Pacific, and the Occidental and Oriental steamship companies were to blame for increased Japanese immigration. Kearney attributed the "mass" unemployment of girls and boys to the influx of Japanese, who would work for six months or a year for their clothes and the privilege of attending school. "After school they would walk down the street with American girls ... white girls should not be permitted to associate with [Japanese]."⁶

At the same time Kearney was giving speeches against Japanese, the San Francisco Call launched a series of articles in which Japanese were characterized as polite, courteous, smiling, and "nobody ever has occasion to kick or cuff them, or even to upbraid them ... but they are taking work away from our boys and girls and away from our men and women."⁷ Again, it is stated Japanese work for "next to nothing ... they will take anything they get in way of compensation. In this way they displace thousands of white girls and boys as domestics or in factories."⁸ The paper reported that Japanese women, hardly to be seen six years previously, have taken "exclusive possession of St. Mary's street, where they bold forth without restraint by the police and hail every passer-by with the familiar cry of the siren."⁹

The Call then asked if the state could afford to draw half or even one-third of Japan's fifty million to its shores? "They are already in nearly every industry and profession, from fowl-raising to photography, from dishwashing to doctoring, and they work very cheaply."¹⁰ Although the paper estimated a Japanese population of 15,000 on the coast, and nearly one-third of these in San Francisco,¹¹ it claimed that people up and down the whole coast were beginning to be alarmed.¹²

---

⁴Sacramento Record Union, July 7, 1892, p. 3/1.

⁵Ibid.

⁶San Francisco Call, May 30, 1892, p. 3/3.

⁷San Francisco Call, May 4, 1892, p. 8/1.

⁸Ibid., p. 1/1.

⁹Ibid.

¹⁰San Francisco Call, May 6, 1892, p. 3/3.

¹¹San Francisco Call, May 4, 1892, p. 1/1.

¹²San Francisco Call, May 18, 1892, p. 3/1.

Much of the immigration, according to the Call, was coming from Hawaii. It added that the "Japs"[13] were packed in the ship's hold like sardines in a box, "as poverty-stricken and ill-favored a set of Mongolians as ever set foot on these shores before the days of the exclusion act."[14] Calling these Japanese "coolies" and "contract laborers," willing to work on California ranches for ten dollars a month, the Call seemed to have aroused little public sentiment for its new-found nativism. When its reporters interviewed the Commissioner of Immigration, the newsmen were informed that Japanese were not declared paupers, and therefore were allowed to come ashore.[15] He also indicated some of the problems of a commissioner:

> By trying to keep out the Japs I antagonize the steamship companies and set the Japanese authorities all to making complaints. On the other hand, if I do not do my duty to the letter the papers will burn me up.[16]

The Call complimented the Commissioner for his "good work" since he had kept 200 Japanese from landing and returned another 200--all of which cost the steamship companies $20,000.

While the Call maintained its watch dog attitude on Japanese immigration in the 1890's, labor groups and patriotic orders seemed willing to carry on the legacy of prejudice already adopted against the Chinese by applying it to Japanese. The American Federation of Labor first passed a resolution in 1892 to restrict Japanese immigration and "endorsing the stand of Pacific Coast unions to put 'cheap Japanese laborers' in the same status as Chinese."[18]

The social treatment of Orientals during the 1890's was destined to change little in the next twenty years. The Native Sons of the Golden West (which by 1920 was one of the most outspoken leaders of Anti-Japanese sentiment), was, in 1893, discriminating against Chinese. Jee Ho, a wealthy Chinese of San Francisco, had formed "Rising Sun Parlor No. 1," with the assistance of C. C. Higgins, a druggist and past master of San Francisco Parlor No. 49. With a membership of 185, the

---

[13]This contraction "first appeared consistently in the columns of the Coast Seamen's Journal during the 1890's," Floyd W. Matson, The Anti-Japanese Movement in California: 1890-1942 (unpublished M.A. Thesis, University of California, Berkeley, 1953), p. 79. Two editors and a contributor to the Journal were Walter Macarthur, Paul Scharrenberg, and Andrew Furuseth (Union Secretary for over 48 years), all of whom were active members in the Asiatic Exclusion League. Cf. I. B. Cross, A History of the Labor Movement in California, pp. 330-331; 169.

[14]San Francisco Call, June 23, 1892, p. 7/5.

[15]San Francisco Call, November 15, 1892, p. 1/7.

[16]San Francisco Call, June 25, 1892, p. 8/1.

[17]San Francisco Call, November 15, 1892, p. 1/7; Call, August 26, 1892, p. 3/5; Call, January 27, 1907, p. 24/1; Call, June 15, 1907, p. 8/1; Call, February 9, 1909, p. 6/1.

[18]Matson, op. cit., p. 6. Since immigrant Orientals could not become citizens, the membership in labor unions was reserved to citizens and those eligible to citizenship; cf. testimony of C. M. Krosen in United States Congress, House of Representatives, Committee on Immigration and Naturalization, Hearings on Japanese Immigration (Washington, 1921), pp. 490-493, hereafter cited as Hearings on Japanese Immigration, 1920.

Chinese applied to the Grand Parlor for a charter.[19] The Native Sons pointed out that the constitution of the order forbade the admittance of any but white members. "Why, the boys have been laughing heartily at their fatuity and look upon it as the latest Mongolian joke. It looks as if the Chinese had not much sense of humor to take all this trouble for something impossible for them to obtain."[20] A similar type of discrimination was used with regard to the Japanese in Los Angeles.

> At the Grace Methodist Church in Los Angeles, on May 15 [1888], another YMCA was organized. This was the Japanese Young Men's Christian Association whose membership jumped from the original eight to twenty in a few weeks. According to The Watchman, [the association's semimonthly international medium of communication], this Japanese association was the second formed in the United States. Having adopted a separate constitution and bylaws, based upon suggestions of the International Committee for Associations in Small Towns, it could not be considered a branch or even a part of the first-established Los Angeles YMCA.[21]

The fear of "cheap" Oriental labor was a concept applied to Chinese and Japanese alike. It seems that some white farm workers objected to "unfair" competition and economic displacement. It was these first attacks against the Japanese that "fastened upon them a cheap-labor stereotype which was never effectively eradicated."[22]

Near the turn of the century, an incident occurred in Johannesburg and Randsburg, two small mining towns near the eastern boundary of Kern County, which involved two Japanese students, Fotaro Nagata and Chitose Suzuki, Governor Budd, the District Attorney of Kern County (Alvin Fay); and the head of the Japanese legation in Washington, Taru Hoshi.[23]

The controversy was precipitated by the proprietor of the Hotel Johannesburg, Mrs. H. L. Squires, when she hired a Japanese chef and waiter "... bright, brainy little fellows, who are educating themselves in this country, and are strictly first-class servants."[24] The Japanese were hired through an employment agency in Los Angeles, which, according to Mrs. Squires, could not obtain white laborers for employment in mining country at that time of year.

---

[19]San Francisco Call, February 4, 1893, p. 8/1.

[20]San Francisco Call, February 5, 1893, p. 6/2. The official Journal of the Native Sons, the Grizzly Bear, maintained the fraternal order was organized "To Hold California For the White Race" while it stood for "Absolute Toleration" and "complete Americanization"; cf. the back covers of the Grizzly Bear, September 1923-October 1925.

[21]Theodore Grivas, "A History of the Los Angeles Young Men's Christian Association: The First Twenty Years," California Historical Society Quarterly, XLIV (September 1965), 7. It should be emphasized that leading members of the YMCA by 1920 had joined with the non-nativistic groups; cf. American Committee of Justice, California and The Japanese (Oakland, California), p. 1 ff.

[22]Matson, op. cit., p. 48.

[23]The following correspondence will be found in Governor Budd's papers (GP6: 117-121), 1897, MS, California State Archives, Sacramento. The governor had asked Fay and his secretary, Peter J. Shields, to gather information for a full investigation.

[24]Letters, Mrs. H. L. Squires to Alvin Fay, July 2, 1897, MS, Budd Papers, GP6: 119.

When the Japanese passed through Randsburg, about a mile from Johannesburg, "angry mutterings were heard in the camp."[25] Couriers were dispatched to Johannesburg to learn if the residents of that camp "sanctioned the infringement of the rights of white laborers."[26] A joint committee of the citizens of the two camps was called by the following notice which was posted in the two camps:

> Notice is hereby given to all miners, mine-owners and all persons interested in the welfare of the camps of Randsburg and Johannesburg to meet at the Hallenbeck restaurant in Randsburg this (Monday) evening, May 31 at 8 o'clock to discuss and look after the protection of the white labor of aforesaid camps.
>
> By Order of the Committee.[27]

A committee of five (two from Johannesburg and 3 from Randsburg) was appointed to inform Mrs. Squires that the Japanese must go without the slightest delay. According to the Call, the committee discussed the matter in a "peaceable and businesslike manner."[28] Mrs. Squires claimed the right of a law abiding citizen in a free country to employ those who could most satisfactorily do her work.

> They said no cheap labor could come in here. I said I pay them just the same as I did the white help, and in return get an equivalent for my money. These Japs are not miners--simply house servants, and will never interfere with any of you. 'Oh,' they said, 'they will start cheap restaurants and hurt your business.' I said that is my affair, and if you get cheap food--all the better for you. They said the Japs must go on the stage to-morrow morning.[29]

Mr. Sloan, who was employed by Mrs. Squires, asked the committee if the demand was really a threat, and the chairman of the committee said that it was. Then, Mr. Sloan said, "I defy you individually and collectively."[30] The committee responded that another "mass meeting" would be called and would report their findings the next night. Mr. Sloan went to Randsburg to seek assistance and protection for the Japanese.

---

[25]Letter, William R. Day, Assistant Secretary to John Sherman, Secretary of State to Governor Budd, June 17, 1897, MS, Budd Papers, RG6: 117. Also contains a reprint of the San Francisco Call, June 1, 1897. The San Francisco Call article pointed out that Goler, the principal camp in the area before Randsburg, excluded Chinese. "One of the rules agreed upon there was that any Chinaman who dared visit the camp would be given twenty minutes in which to retreat his steps, or made to pay one dollar for every minute thereafter spent in Goler."

[26]Ibid., p. 2.

[27]Ibid., p. 3.

[28]Ibid., p. 4.

[29]Letter, Mrs. Squires to Alvin Fay, July 2, 1897, Budd Papers, GP6: 119.

[30]Ibid.

The constable of Randsburg, Claude Bahannon, claimed that Mrs. Squires applied for "Chinamen" as employees, and that the two Japanese "... were the first coolies ever in this district and naturally the whole population was indignant."[31]

When the committee returned on May 31, it was accompanied by what Mrs. Squires called twenty-nine hobos and mob-outlaws,

> Some were Irish, and some were perhaps miners but I know the Chairman, Finch, had dug a hole about three feet deep when he instigated this trouble, so his feelings as a miner should not have been deeply hurt.[32]

The committee informed her that she would have forty-eight hours in which to get other help, and that it would be unwise to keep the Japanese after that time, as they would be taken out, and her property might suffer.[33] As the reporter for the Call saw it,

> Had the offender been a man, instead of a woman there would have been no further mincing of words; the employer of Japanese would have been summarily dealt with, and the coolies would have been in luck if they escaped with unpunctured cuticles.[34]

A subscription was taken up by the committee to reimburse Mrs. Squires for the cost of the Japaneses' fare from Los Angeles and to pay the return fare.[35] When the stage arrived at the hotel, the Japanese "started away each one of them with a big carving knife in their hands. Mr. Sloan went with them and staid [sic] until they were out of Randsburg."[36]

Mrs. Squires obtained two white cooks after the Japanese left and both turned out to be drunkards within a week. The two Negroes that followed the whites "have no brains." Exclaiming that her business had been seriously affected, she hoped the incident would "not drift into cheap politics, but remain a United States Affair and the Japs get justice."[37]

---

[31] Letter, Claude Bahannon, Constable of Randsburg, to Alvin Fay, June 29, 1897, Budd Papers, GP6: 118. He maintained "that it was the edict of the people generally that there should be no Japs or Chinese allowed in the camp."

[32] Letter, Mrs. Squires to Alvin Fay, July 2, 1897, Budd Papers, GP6: 119.

[33] Ibid. The constable claimed that "no violence or threats were used, as I was on hand to see that everything was all right." Letter, Bahannon to Fay, June 29, 1897, Budd Papers, GP6: 118.

[34] Letter, William R. Day to Governor Budd, June 17, 1897, Budd Papers, GP6: 117, p. 4. The Japanese were locked in the kitchen of the hotel and "the white laborers of the hostelry stood guard to defend them in case the miners decided to eject them by force." Ibid., p. 5.

[35] Letter, Bahannon to Fay, June 29, 1897, Budd Papers, GP6: 118.

[36] Letter, Mrs. Squires to Fay, July 2, 1897, Budd Papers, GP6: 119. As Constable Bahannon expressed it: "I don't think the Japs objected to leaving."

[37] Ibid.

The Constable of Randsburg, who seems to have backed the "joint" committee and who stated that no threats had been made, in turn seemed to threaten the Governor. "Please call Governor Budd's attention to the fact that it was Estee's being a Chinese lover that he [Budd] now holds the position of Governor."[38]

The Japanese legation in Washington complained of the treatment of the Japanese servants and asked that "the necessary steps may be taken to prevent the recurrence of similar violations of the law and the rights of Japanese subjects resident in this country."[39]

Anti-Oriental sentiment, then, tended to appear in those areas such as San Francisco and Randsburg because certain individuals seemed to believe that Chinese and Japanese represented "cheap" and over-competitive labor. It is equally important to assert that there were other areas and other people in California who viewed Oriental labor, whether "cheap" or not, as an asset to the state's agriculture.[40]

The Sacramento Daily Union in June 18, 1869, reflected an early and favorable impression of Japanese near Gold Hill, El Dorado County, and in Alameda County where they were earning "a very respectable living by agriculture and horticulture."[41]

> It is the interest of California to welcome and encourage these immigrants. To repel them as Senator Casserly would the Chinese is just senseless and barbarous ... and it is singular, too, that these modern statesmen ground their aversion to the asiatics upon the same objections which the savage Indians urged against the whites--color and dissimilarity of habits ... there is probably much knowledge in the possession of these Asiatics that we could profit from, to compensate us in some measure for our sufferings from the very enlightened prejudice against their coppery color. They will at all events teach us how to produce tea and silk, some useful lessons in frugality, industry, and possibly in politeness.[42]

Such a favorable impression of Japanese appeared in the Sacramento Bee shortly after the beginning of the Twentieth Century. In response to questions from farmers and fruit growers about the increased Japanese population, Professor Fowler stated

---

[38]Letter, Bahannon to Fay, June 29, 1897, Budd Papers, GP6: 118.

[39]Letter, Taru Hoshi to John Sherman, Secretary of State, June 16, 1897, Budd Papers, GP6: 117.

[40]The State Labor Commissioner's Report, 1909, by J. D. Mackenzie, surveyed 4,102 farms in thirty-six counties and showed there was a need and a desire for Japanese labor. Cf. Sidney L. Gulick, The American Japanese Problem, Appendix B, pp. 316-323; and the Appendix to the Journal of the Senate and Assembly of the 40th Session of the Legislature of the State of California, "Report of the Bureau of Labor Statistics," III, 1913, pp. 604-637.

[41]Sacramento Daily Union, June 18, 1869, p. 2/1.

[42]Ibid.

that he did not believe the danger was as great as some had imagined. As a citizen he felt no fear, "when I cease to be an American citizen, I will then be afraid."[43]

Despite the Bee's warning of increased Japanese immigration and Oriental control of the berry district,[44] the Japanese continued to settle in Florin because the Caucasian found that renting land to the Japanese was a profitable, financial investment. As one land owner commented, "I have rented to the Japanese ninety acres at five dollars per acre cash rent, making $450 per year, without doing a stroke. With hard work and long hours, I used to net about $135 per year."[45] Japanese farmers were welcome because "White men will not do this work, and I don't blame them; therefore, we much accept the Japanese--the only help available, or go out of business."[46]

The first Japanese to rent land in Florin, Charlie May, began planting strawberries in 1893. In less than ten years, it was found that

> About 87 percent of the acreage is, in a manner, under the control of the Japanese ... this condition would appear to militate against white labor, and give the impression that this section is a poor place for white men to come to for the purpose of engaging in strawberry growing .... Facts and figures go to prove that at no time during the existence of this harmonious settlement have the conditions been more favorable for all classes of people than they are at the present time .... The man who has money, and wishes to make big interest, can buy bare land at from $25 to $70 per acre, and rent it to the Japanese at a cash rent of $5 per acre per year.[47]

It is important to point out that Japanese labor was not only desired, but was welcome in the Florin district in the beginning of the first decade of the Twentieth Century. Both the Bee and its associate editor, Valintine S. McClatchy, were to take an entirely opposite view of these people by the end of the second decade.[48] Indeed, it seems likely that Anti-Japanese sentiment received its main impetus from

---

[43] Sacramento Bee, January 31, 1902, p. 5.

[44] Sacramento Bee, February 10, 1902, p. 4.

[45] Sacramento Bee, April 5, 1902, p. 15.

[46] G. Cox, ed., Sacramento Bee, March 29, 1902, p. 15.

[47] Ibid. This article is about identical to the one published on April 5, which included a list of Japanese farmers in Florin.

[48] Cf. Testimony of V. S. McClatchy in Hearings on Japanese Immigration, 1920, pp. 206-215; 220-244; 281-284; 338-346. The Florin District was cited over and over again by the labor unions and newspapers as one of the best examples that Japanese intended to drive out the white man; cf., A. E. L. Proceedings, April 12, 1908, p. 7. Hiram Johnson once commented that he was pleased to hear that Secretary of State, W. J. Bryan, had accepted an invitation to see Florin, since it was "California's best argument for an anti alien land law." San Francisco Call, May 1, 1913, p. 2/4. A more objective view may be found in H. A. Millis', Japanese Problems in the United States, Chapters 5 and 7. The Japanese view of Florin may be found in the San Francisco Chronicle, January 16, 1918, pp. 17-24; January 15, 1919, pp. 17-23; and January 14, 1920, pp. 37-48.

the urban areas, most especially from San Francisco, where anti-Oriental sentiment had a history of protestors and a ready audience. San Francisco politicians and labor leaders were instigators and perpetuators of anti-Japanese sentiment.

One of the more effective "propaganda devices" they used was the staging of public mass meetings or a "monster rally" at which the Chinese or Japanese were attacked as Asiatic hordes flooding the state with cheap labor.[49] What has been cited as the first mass meeting held in San Francisco to seek "protection against Asiatic hordes" and to "protect against the Japanese" was held on May 7, 1900.[50] The meeting, held largely in response to demands from the labor press, featured addresses emphasizing the grievances of labor. Presided over by Walter Macarthur of the Seamen's Union and the San Francisco Labor Council, the speakers included Mayor James D. Phelan, Patrick H. McCarthy of the Building Trades Council, and Professor Edward A. Ross, a sociologist at Stanford University.[51]

Mayor James D. Phelan had previously shown an interest in Anti-Japanese sentiment. In March of 1900, he and the Board of Supervisors quarantined the Chinese and Japanese sections, but not any other part of the city. The San Francisco Chronicle on May 30 charged Phelan with playing the "role of a fakir" and that stories of a plague were circulated purely for political purposes.[52] The Chronicle made a similar charge in 1920 while Phelan, as senior Senator, was campaigning for re-election. In an effort to deny the Chronicle's accusation that Phelan had re-instigated anti-Japanese sentiment to gain re-election, Edward L. Fitzgerald gave testimony to what may have been Phelan's first interest in anti-Japanese propaganda.

> I hear reports of political propaganda by opponents of Senator Phelan to the effect that he discovered the Japanese problem just prior to this campaign .... Few people, however, are aware of his deep and long continued interest in this work. None, perhaps, know that it was Senator Phelan who financed the first investigation of Japanese immigration, which was undertaken by the State of California twenty-five years ago while the late James H. Budd was governor.
>
> During 1895, I, as State Labor Commissioner, established the first state free employment bureau, and it was then that the public attention was first drawn to the influx of Japanese labor. In that year I estimated there were 10,000 Japanese in the state,

---

[49]Matson, op. cit., pp. 7, 18. Cf. Coolidge, op. cit., pp. 243-244; and San Francisco Call, December 24, 1906, p. 1/4.

[50]Matson, loc. cit.; R. L. Buell, "The Development of the Anti-Japanese Agitation in the United States, I," Political Science Quarterly, XXXVII (1922), 605-638.

[51]Matson, loc. cit.; A. E. L. Proceedings, January 1908, p. 7. One of Ross's comments was "that the guns of war ships of this government better be trained on any ships bringing Japanese to this shore rather than permit the Oriental to land." Such statements caused Mrs. Stanford to regard Professor Ross as "dangerous"; while David S. Jordan believed him to be "a happy-go-lucky-boy." San Francisco Chronicle, January 22, 1911, p. 1/4.

[52]Buell, op. cit., p. 633. In November of 1901 as Mayor of San Francisco and a candidate for Senatorship, Phelan called a convention "to frame a memorial to Congress for re-enactment of Chinese exclusion," Coolidge, loc. cit.

> who were a source of irritation to white labor, as the Japanese were working for about $15 a month. The facts demanded an investigation and report.
>
> There were no funds available for the work and I personally made appeal to Mr. Phelan, then a private citizen, for I knew his attitude on the subject of Japanese immigration.
>
> I hesitate to state the amounts he gave me. Let it suffice to say that he offered more than I would accept and that the share of the State toward bearing the expense of myself and staff was entered in the financial report at only $47, an exhaustive report was prepared and is printed as an official record of the State, and $47 does not go very far.
>
> Senator Phelan made these donations without ostentation and has probably forgotten them. I take pleasure in recalling them when I hear it said that he discovered the Japanese peril only six months before he came before the voters for re-election as United States Senator.[53]

The Seventh Biennial Report of the Bureau of Labor Statistics in 1896 contains twenty-five pages under the title "Japanese Labor." It can hardly be considered as objective when it contains such distortions as "... the Jap is inately [sic] and hereditarily unreliable, and is not to be depended upon at any time."[54]

The report indicates that Japanese had quietly moved into the farming and fruit-growing districts and attracted little attention until laborers "in traveling from place to place, seeking employment were refused same, while gangs of Japanese were busily engaged performing the work that they had hitherto been given."[55]

The anti-Japanese sentiment evident in the Seventh Biennial Report, appeared in succeeding reports as the Ninth Biennial of 1900, rhetorically states, "Would white labor be paid more for such work if the competition of Chinese and Japanese labor was eliminated? It is likely that in many cases it would."[56]

Combined with the Bureau of Labor Statistics, politicians, labor and civic leaders, as well as the Call's anti-Japanese sentiment, the legacy of prejudice against the Chinese was to profoundly influence sentiment against Japanese immigration. It is not surprising that San Francisco, having led the anti-Chinese movement, was the locale for the first organized opposition to Japanese.

---

[53]Los Angeles Evening Herald, November 1, 1920, p. 10/5. Walter Macarthur, as well as James Phelan, took an interest in the Bureau of Labor Statistics. Cf. Tenth Biennial Report, 1901-1902, p. 9.

[54]Seventh Biennial Report of the Bureau of Labor Statistics, 1895-1896, p. 126. Cf. I. B. Cross, op. cit., p. 264.

[55]Ibid., p. 102.

[56]Ninth Biennial Report of the Bureau of Labor Statistics, 1899-1900, p. 32.

CHAPTER II

THE ASIATIC EXCLUSION LEAGUE: ITS FORMATION,
AGITATION, AND EXPANSION, 1905-1909

You may make up your minds that this fight must be kept up for years before we get real Asiatic exclusion. We may be able to gain further ground in the next Congress, but it will take years of energetic and intelligent work to raise barriers against the Oriental hordes sufficiently strong and high enough to protect the people of California and American civilization from the evil that has been menacing our country from across the Pacific for the last forty years ....

It may be that the present Congress and the next, and that this President will not, but the votes of the people of the United States will sometime elect a Congress and a President who will give us a Japanese exclusion law which will protect and preserve the United States as a white man's country.

    Olaf Andrew Tveitmoe, San Francisco Call, January 16, 1907,
    p. 5/11; and May 13, 1907, p. 7/3.

Every man and woman in California will know the truth about the Japanese question, but they will not learn it through the press.

    Mayor Eugene Schmitz, San Francisco Call, March 7, 1907,
    p. 3/6.

CHAPTER II

THE ASIATIC EXCLUSION LEAGUE: ITS FORMATION,
AGITATION, AND EXPANSION, 1905-1909

During the first years of the Twentieth Century, the embryonic labor unions of San Francisco put forth what was to be the first effectively organized effort in opposition to the Japanese. The Union Labor Party, perhaps one of the strongest political unions in California during the first decade, was formed in September 1901. One of its planks "called for the establishment of segregated schools for Asiatics."[1] Indeed, Asiatic exclusion planks were maintained in the Union Labor Party through the election of 1909,[2] while at the same time, the California State Federation of Labor reiterated its desire to extend the Chinese Exclusion Act to "other Asiatics."[3]

Of more lasting consequence to the California nativist movement were the San Francisco newspapers and the labor journals. The San Francisco Building Trades Council, an affiliate of the American Federation of Labor, founded its newspaper, Organized Labor, in 1900. The editor, Olaf A. Tveitmoe, was also the Secretary of the San Francisco Building Trades Council and held both positions for over twenty years.[4] The paper's second issue in March 1900, stated the "blabbering, pretentious, half-civilized Japanese were fast supplanting white workmanship both in field and factory, while driving American girls into the stifling beer joints and the gloomy streets; into the bawdy-houses and slums of the tenderloin district and the Barbary Coast."[5] The following year, during March, Tveitmoe began a series

---

[1]Edward J. Rowell, The Union Labor Party of San Francisco, 1901-1911 (Unpublished Dissertation, University of California, Berkeley, 1938), p. 31. It has been stated that the Union Labor Party was principally responsible for the Japanese School Segregation Act of 1906, Floyd W. Matson, The Anti-Japanese Movement in California: 1890-1942, p. 11.

[2]Ibid., pp. 195, 214. In 1907, the Union Labor platform stated: "Believing that our American workmen should not be compelled to compete with Japanese or Chinese labor, we favor the enlargement of the Chinese Exclusion Act, so that it may apply to all classes of Asiatics, especially Japanese, and urge that it may be perpetual in its application." On the same platform is another plank which seems incongruous to the above: "We earnestly deplore any agitation or legislation that would tend to array class against class or cause prejudice due to religion, social, or financial differences," San Francisco Call, September 29, 1907, p. 2/5.

[3]Matson, op. cit., p. 6. The State Labor Commissioner in 1900 received returns from 217 unions containing 37,500 members. About forty-one percent were in San Francisco, I. B. Cross, A History of the Labor Movement in California, p. 228.

[4]Frederick L. Ryan, Industrial Relations in the San Francisco Building Trades, p. 33, note 29; I. B. Cross, op. cit., p. 338, note 26.

[5]Matson, op. cit., p. 5.

of articles "warning against the competitive danger of the Japanese, urging their incorporation within the Chinese Exclusion Law, and calling for public action to limit immigration."[6]

The San Francisco Labor Council and its publication, The Labor Clarion, carried on a campaign demanding restrictive legislation against the evils of Japanese competition. The California State Federation of Labor in 1904 adopted the San Francisco Labor Council's warning that increased numbers of Japanese and Korean laborers would "present a problem of race preservation ... which can only be solved through a policy exclusion."[7]

It was not until May 1905, that the Japanese and Korean Exclusion League was formed out of the San Francisco labor unions. In the earlier part of the year, the Chronicle and Organized Labor seemed to have intensified agitation for an exclusion league. In February, the Chronicle warned its readers of a brown stream of Japanese immigration which was likely to become an "inundating torrent."[8] Tveitmoe warned the building trades members on March 11, of a "peaceful invasion" of Japan's discharged soldiers from the Russo-Japanese War.

> Drunk with victory and fired by uncontrollable ambition, these one million Japanese Napoleons will turn their eyes around for new territory to conquer. The United States, and California in particular, is an inviting field, and if they can capture it without power or shell, so much the better.[9]

In the same issue of Organized Labor, Tveitmoe culminated his two month appeal for the formation of an anti-Japanese society. In order to give the exclusion gospel the appearance of civic solidarity he asked that the "league be composed of delegates from all central labor bodies, mercantile associations, clubs and other civic bodies."[10]

---

[6]Matson, op. cit., p. 5. The Coast Seamen's Journal rejoined the anti-Japanese agitation on April 25, 1901. The founder of the paper, Andrew Furuseth, "had a small core of disciples who were intellectuals like himself--Walter Macarthur and Paul Scharrenberg," Richard H. Dillon, Shanghaiing Days, p. 300. All three Scandinavian immigrant "intellectuals" were contributors to the Journal as well as delegates to the Asiatic Exclusion League.

[7]Matson, op. cit., pp. 6-7. See also San Francisco Call, November 16, 1904, p. 3/1; and November 19, 1904, p. 3/7.

[8]San Francisco Chronicle, February 23, 1905, p. 1/3; I. B. Cross, op. cit., p. 265.

[9]Matson, op. cit., p. 85.

[10]Ibid., p. 9. Such an ideal was not realized until 1919 when a large number of civic and patriotic associations joined the labor unions on a state-wide basis.

The first formal meeting of the league took place on May 7, 1905.[11] The *Chronicle* reported that the convention had been called by O. A. Tveitmoe of the Building Trades Council with delegates from labor unions, civic and commercial bodies from all over the State with the purpose of protesting "against the unrestricted immigration of Chinese and will have a strong bearing upon the anti-Asiatic agitation which is gaining ground all over the country."[12] The *Call* stated that thousands of representatives from the cities' labor unions were present with hundreds of "others."[13] Addresses were given by Walter Macarthur, Mayor Schmitz, Andrew Furuseth, Will J. French, and Senator Edward I. Wolfe, all of whom urged "a vigorous campaign against the yellow peril in speeches that resounded with eloquence and determination."[14] Chairman Tveitmoe's speech was perhaps the most persuasive in instigating fear of an invasion by Japanese soldiers.

> The Japanese would Mongolize America if they were given the chance. We should not forget our civilization and throw discretion to the winds out of recognition of the valor of the Jap in the present war. They will become a scourge to the country. In time of war, pest or famine, they die like flies, but in prosperous times they will multiply at a rate that would astound one. Don't be deceived, Japanese progress and energy are deceptive.[15]

Once a year, usually during the annual meeting in May, the Exclusion League[16] would elect its officers and members of the executive committee. The League's

---

[11] Raymond A. Esthus, *Theodore Roosevelt and Japan*, p. 130; Buell, "The Development of anti-Japanese Agitation," p. 617; Thomas A. Bailey, *Theodore Roosevelt and the Japanese--American Crisis*, p. 15; Roger Daniels, *The Politics of Prejudice*, pp. 27-28, 126. Daniels dates the League's formation from May 14, 1905, since the May 7th meeting formed no actual organizational structure. O. A. Tveitmoe considered May 7 as the founding date of the League, cf. A. E. L., *Proceedings*, February 3, 1908, pp. 18, 19.

[12] *San Francisco Chronicle*, May 8, 1905, p. 1/1.

[13] *San Francisco Call*, May 8, 1905, p. 2/2. Invitations were sent o Senators Bard, Perkins, several congressmen, and Governor Pardee. None of these leaders were present. The *Sacramento Bee*, in a small article, stated there would be "two hundred organizations present ... attended by delegates from trade unions, improvement clubs, civic and political societies," May 6, 1905, p. 10/3.

[14] *San Francisco Call*, May 8, 1905, p. 2/1.

[15] Ibid., p. 2/3.

[16] From May 1905, until March 1908, the League's title was the Japanese and Korean Exclusion League, cf. *San Francisco Call*, March 9, 1908, p. 5/4. However, within the month, the League had changed its name to The Asiatic Exclusion League, cf. *San Francisco Call*, March 29, 1908, p. 38/7. Reasons for this change are not entirely clear, but one of the reasons may have been the league's general desire to expand Chinese Exclusion to all other Asiatics--not just the Japanese and Koreans. Another cause might have been the Report of The Commissioner-General for the fiscal year ended June 30, 1907, which showed a total of 39 immigrant Koreans, cf. Sixth Annual Report of the Secretary of Commerce and Labor, *The Report of The Commissioner-General of Immigration*, 1908, p. 82. The *San Francisco Call*, December 16, 1907, p. 2/3, published many of the figures from the immigration reports. No mention is made of Koreans and all attention was focused on Japanese figures. The League may have changed its name to "Asiatic" in order to avoid

officers--President, O. A. Tveitmoe; Vice President, E. B. Carr;[17] and Secretary-Treasurer, A. E. Yoell[18] did not change throughout the existence of the League.[19] The Executive Committee which changed from year to year, contained some of the most prominent labor leaders of San Francisco. Members of the committee included: Senator Frank McGowan,[20] Walter Macarthur, C. F. Knight,[21] George B. Benham,[22] F. W. Brandis, J. B. Bowen,[23] J. D. Nagel,[24] John I. Nolan,[25] Michael Casey,

mentioning only the Japanese and perhaps further increasing the wrath of President Roosevelt. Roger Daniels states "the organization was called the Japanese and Korean Exclusion League until December 1907," The Politics of Prejudice, p. 126, note 34.

[17] Carr was the delegate from the Improvement Clubs of San Francisco, San Francisco Call, October 23, 1905, p. 12/1. However, while Tveitmoe was being held in jail during 1913, Carr posted $12,500 as part of the bail. The paper listed Carr as a "blacksmith," San Francisco Call, January 16, 1913, p. 4/2.

[18] An electrician by trade, Yoell was a close friend and associate of Tveitmoe, cf. A. E. Yoell, "Oriental vs. American Labor," The Annals of the American Academy of Social and Political Science, XXXIV (September 1909), 247-256; San Francisco Call, January 15, 1908, p. 3/3; San Francisco Call, September 20, 1908, p. 8/1.

[19] San Francisco Call, August 14, 1905, p. 7/5; San Francisco Call, May 20, 1912, p. 14/7.

[20] McGowan spoke at a number of rallies on the exclusion effort and helped Tveitmoe establish a branch League in Stockton, A. E. L., Proceedings, May 10, 1908, pp. 4-5. McGowan and Tveitmoe worked with Theodore A. Bell to draft a bill for Congress to exclude all Asiatics, San Francisco Call, March 11, 1907, p. 2/6; San Francisco Call, June 19, 1911, p. 12/6.

[21] Knight was the United States Shipping Commissioner in San Francisco until April 1913, when Macarthur was appointed to the job by President Wilson. Macarthur commented, "The appointment comes as a complete surprise to me," San Francisco Call, April 26, 1913, p. 16/2; San Francisco Call, April 30, 1913, p. 2/4.

[22] Many of these League members gave speeches before various associations to further expand the League's influence, cf. Benham's speech to the members of the Social Science League, San Francisco Call, July 27, 1908, p. 12/2. Benham was the President of the San Francisco Labor Council; Secretary of the State Federation of Labor; and the Chairman of the Law and Legislation Committee for the San Francisco Labor Council. Benham, like Tveitmoe, was quite outspoken in his anti-Japanese sentiment: "But no such outlook is possible when contemplating the influx of the wiry, under-sized, arrogant, mischief-making and dishonest Japanese. Their customs, beliefs, habits, their standards of morality and living are all intensely and permanently inimical to ours," San Francisco Call, January 6, 1907, p. 51/1-3.

[23] While a delegate to the Exclusion League, Bowen was the business agent for the Alameda County Building Trades Council as well as the Vice President of the International Council of the Wood, Wire and Metal Lathers' Union of the United States and Canada, San Francisco Call, February 26, 1907, p. 4/6. He later became the First Vice President of the State Building Trades Council, San Francisco Call, August 9, 1910, p. 4/5. He was temporarily "ousted" by the trades council when it was found that he had agreed to deliver the solid union labor vote of

Andrew Furuseth, William R. Hagerty, Charles H. Parker, F. Sullivan, R. A. A. Summers, W. A. Cole, P. J. O'Shea, J. J. O'Neill,[26] H. F. McMahon,[27] Senator Marc Anthony,[28] and a number of other members who served on the committee.[29] One can assume that membership and participation in the Exclusion League aired the aspirations to better paying and more prestigious employment.

Perhaps the most important man to be consistently re-elected to the Executive Committee was P. H. McCarthy. (The P. H. for Patrick Henry was interpreted by his opponents as "Pin Head."[30]) He was the President of the San Francisco Building Trades Council for twenty-four years, President of the State Building Trades Council for over twenty years, and Mayor of San Francisco from 1909 to 1911.[31] McCarthy was a close friend and advisor to his Secretary-Treasurer in the Building Trades Council, Olaf Andrew Tveitmoe. Their social, political and business friendship was to last throughout their careers.[32]

Oakland to Dr. F. F. Jackson, candidate for Mayor of the Independent or Citizens Ticket, *San Francisco Examiner*, February 27, 1909, p. 4/1.

[24]Nagel, it seems, became the Secretary of the Department of Commerce and Labor. A. E. Yoell, in a letter to President Taft, complained of Nagel's attempts to "oust Daniel J. Keefe as Commissioner-General of Immigration, with the intention of promoting to the office one of his personal friends," *San Francisco Call*, February 27, 1913, p. 18/4.

[25]Nolan was the legislative agent for the San Francisco Labor Council, A. E. L., *Proceedings*, January 17, 1909, p. 3; *San Francisco Call*, December 28, 1910, p. 4/6. He was also the Secretary of the Labor Council and United States Congressman by 1920, cf. F. L. Ryan, *op. cit.*, p. 208.

[26]Joseph J. O'Neill (like Tveitmoe, Scharrenberg, Macarthur, and French), was an editor. On February 28, 1902, the San Francisco Labor Council began its weekly publication of the *Labor Clarion* which O'Neill edited until his death in 1908 when he was succeeded by Will J. French, I. B. Cross, *op. cit.*, p. 339.

[27]McMahon was the President of the Anti-Jap Laundry League at the same time he was a member of the Executive Committee of the Asiatic Exclusion League, *San Francisco Call*, February 9, 1909, p. 2/3. After the Asiatic Exclusion League became ineffective by 1913, McMahon carried on the exclusion effort through "coordinating" groups called The Associated Anti-Japanese Leagues, cf. Matson, *op. cit.*, p. 10.

[28]Anthony was one of the League's most outspoken representatives in the State Senate, A. E. L., *Proceedings*, December 20, 1908, p. 21; *op. cit.*, May 15, 1910, p. 18; *San Francisco Call*, May 22, 1911, p. 5/3; *San Francisco Call*, November 18, 1912, p. 4/5.

[29]For a list of other delegates on the Executive Committee, cf. the following: *San Francisco Call*, August 14, 1905, p. 7/5; *San Francisco Call*, May 13, 1907, p. 7/3; *San Francisco Examiner*, May 13, 1907, p. 4/6; *San Francisco Call*, May 11, 1908, p. 7/5; *San Francisco Call*, May 17, 1909, p. 5/4; *San Francisco Call*, May 23, 1911, p. 5/3; *San Francisco Call*, May 20, 1912, p. 14/7.

[30]Louis Adamic, *Dynamite*, p. 201. The *San Francisco Argonaut* described McCarthy as "a blatant bulldozer" and an organizer who conducted the simplest negotiation with the exhibition of physical and vocal energy adequate to the management of a twenty-mule team, *ibid*.

[31]McCarthy's career is briefly summarized in the following: I. B. Cross, *op. cit.*, pp. 246-247; 336-337. E. J. Rowell, *op. cit.*, pp. 204-205. Tveitmoe wrote some

O. A. Tveitmoe may be considered the chief agitator against the Japanese until the passage of the first Alien Land Law in May of 1913.[33] However, very little has been written about him, especially his involvement in the League.[34] Under Tveitmoe's and McCarthy's leadership, the League formulated its main goals and organization in 1905-1906. To accomplish the purpose of the League, four committees were devised: Organization, Finance, Statistics, and Publicity-Printing.

The Committee on Organization was instructed to obtain the full cooperation of the Pacific Coast in the exclusion movement and bring the matter to the notice of Congress.[35] Throughout the eight years of its existence, the League's major

---

of the early history and activities of the Building Trades Council, San Francisco Call, September 3, 1906, p. 14/4. As a candidate for Mayor of San Francisco in 1909, the San Francisco Call interviewed him on his past career. McCarthy made no mention of the Asiatic Exclusion League. The reporter summarized that "He may not make the best mayor San Francisco has ever had. He is the first mayor that can say he made himself mayor," cf. San Francisco Call, July 31, 1909, p. 9/1; San Francisco Call, March 7, 1910, p. 6/6.

[32] San Francisco Call, November 25, 1907, p. 12/1; San Francisco Call, December 31, 1911, p. 18/2; San Francisco Call, January 16, 1913, p. 4/2; San Francisco Call, March 20, 1923, p. 12/1. It is interesting to note that upon Tveitmoe's death, the newspapers made no mention of his participation in the Asiatic Exclusion League, cf. San Francisco Examiner, March 20, 1923, p. 4/3; San Francisco Chronicle, March 20, 1923, p. 3/6-7; Sacramento Bee, March 20, 1923, p. 4/4.

[33] James B. Kessler in 1957 interviewed Franklin Hichborn and Paul Scharrenberg, both of whom were writers for newspapers and labor journals. Both men had known Tveitmoe, cf. Kessler, The Political Factors in California's Anti Alien Land Legislation, 1912-1913, Stanford University, 1958, pp. 27-28; 35-36. F. L. Ryan comments that Tveitmoe "was the moving spirit in the organization of the Asiatic Exclusion League in 1904 and was its president for many years," F. L. Ryan, op. cit., p. 23, note 29.

[34] The following writers have condensed their materials on Tveitmoe into footnotes or brief citations: K. K. Kawakami, The Real Japanese Question; Rowell, op. cit., pp. 146, 148, 163; Ryan, op. cit., pp. 32, 33, 51; Cross, op. cit., pp. 338, note 26, 284; Adamic, op. cit., pp. 216-217, 244-246; Samuel Gompers, Seventy Years of Life and Labor, pp. 165-166, 191-192. Cf. also, Men Who Made San Francisco, 1915, p. 227. The San Francisco Call interviewed Tveitmoe in an article entitled, "Tveitmoe: Man of Big Ambition," San Francisco Call, December 31, 1911, p. 18/2.

[35] San Francisco Call, August 14, 1905, p. 7/5. What may have been the first bill written by the League against Japanese and Koreans and sent to Congress appears in the San Francisco Call, November 27, 1905, p. 12/4-5. The League members determined the best way to get the bill passed was to distribute literature on Asiatic exclusion throughout the Eastern cities while asking the labor unions of those cities to assist them.

goal was the extension of the Chinese exclusion laws to the Japanese.³⁶ The Finance Committee, under the control of P. H. McCarthy, appointed a three man sub-committee to bring the question of finances before the State Federation of Labor and the State Building Trades in January 1906, for the purpose of asking those organizations to contribute one cent per capita of their membership to increase the League's funds. Appearing at the State Federation of Labor in Oakland, Macarthur, McCarthy and Tveitmoe, raised much enthusiasm upon the subject of "Mongolian immigration." The League's resolution requesting the affiliated unions to assess themselves one cent per month per capita to furnish the funds necessary for carrying on the League's propaganda easily passed.³⁸ The per capita tax was also passed in a resolution presented by Tveitmoe the following week at the State Building Trades Council.³⁹ However, at times, the League's finances were not adequate to run the organization.⁴⁰

---

³⁶T. A. Bailey, op. cit., p. 15. Kessler has also stated: "The League was interested in all matters pertaining to Asiatic immigration; its program embraced the promotion of a policy of exclusion by the Federal Government, and secondly, action by the State to discourage the presence of Orientals pending the enactment of the League's panacea--exclusion," J. B. Kessler, op. cit., p. 30.

³⁷San Francisco Call, November 27, 1905, p. 12/5. That the League was in financial straits had been reported by A. E. Yoell a month before. The monthly income of the League was $219, San Francisco Call, October 23, 1905, p. 12/1. The receipts for the year 1906 were $4,675.70, cf. San Francisco Call, May 13, 1907, p. 7/3. The membership of the State Federation of Labor was 36,000, San Francisco Call, January 3, 1906, p. 2/5; while the Building Trades Council of San Francisco was 32,500, San Francisco Call, September 3, 1906, p. 14/1. If these figures are accurate, the League's monthly income would amount to $685 or annually, $8,220. This would indicate that most of the League's finances came from one of these two organizations. It was probably the Building Trades Council since the financial records of the League were stored close to the Building Trades Council's papers in the Metropolis Bank building at Market and New Montgomery; San Francisco Call, January 3, 1912, p. 1/7. Yoell also stated in 1908 that the League received about $12,000 and that 85 percent had been subscribed by the Building Artisans of California, A. E. L., Proceedings, February 3, 1908, p. 55.

³⁸San Francisco Call, January 5, 1906, p. 1/4. The following day, the State Federation of Labor passed resolutions favoring Mongolian exclusion, San Francisco Call, January 7, 1906, p. 43/5; cf. The Oakland Enquirer, January 5, 1906, p. 9/6-7.

³⁹San Francisco Call, January 10, 1906, p. 7/1. A month later Yoell, the League Secretary, stated "that all affiliated labor organizations are practically contributing regularly," San Francisco Call, February 5, 1906, p. 13/4. Tveitmoe never hesitated to use the Building Trades Council conventions as a stump for his anti-Japanese campaign. At the annual convention in 1907, he stated: "I hold that Jordan's generosity has carried away his giant intellect. This is more than a labor problem, it is a race problem, and the benevolent assimilation theory is a miracle that neither he nor any other scientist can hope to achieve. If it could be accomplished, we would have a nation of cutthroats, gaspipe thugs, and human hyenas," San Francisco Call, January 16, 1907, p. 1/3; cf. also San Francisco Call, January 17, 1908, p. 7/3. Such oratory should be compared to what he said at a mass rally the day before Christmas, 1906. "Tveitmoe touched on the doctrine of benevolent assimilation. 'Do you wish to give your daughters in marriage to Chinese and Japanese?' he inquired. 'Do it, and in less than a hundred years you will have a nation of gaspipe thugs and human hyenas .... Give citizenship

The last two committees, Statistics and Publicity-Printing, seemed to have been under the control of the League's Secretary-Treasurer, A. E. Yoell. The most important function of these committees was to spread propaganda throughout the United States against Japanese, and to spread propaganda on the power and effect of the League.[41] The publication of the League's propaganda was handled by the editors of the principal labor journals in San Francisco.[42] At the second annual meeting of the League, Yoell reported the total income for 1906 was $4,675.70, while the expenditures were $4,412.88.

> Much of the money was spent in the publishing of propaganda literature opposing the employment of Chinese coolies on the Panama Canal ... and the support [in Congress] of a measure extending the provisions of the Chinese exclusion act to include Japanese, Koreans and other Asiatics.[43]

Yoell reported that since May 1, 1906, the League had mailed a total of 34,990 pieces of literature in answer to questions of citizens on the exclusion movement.[44] By 1911, the League had published and distributed throughout the country 132,000 pieces of literature for the fiscal year of May 1910 to May 1911.[45]

---

to the Japanese, and you give them your daughters, your homes, your country,'" San Francisco Examiner, December 24, 1906, p. 5/2.

[40]With increases in membership, there seems to have been adequate funds, San Francisco Call, July 15, 1907, p. 11/1. By 1909, the League was addressing communications to labor organizations throughout the United States asking for contributions in small monthly sums to aid the association, San Francisco Call, January 31, 1909, p. 36/2.

[41]The League "engaged in assorted 'research' activities for the purpose of securing statistical support for its political propaganda." Kessler, op. cit., pp. 29-30.

[42]San Francisco Call, October 23, 1905, p. 12/1. The League maintained a "clipping bureau" to compile information for reports, speeches, handbills, journal and editorial propaganda, San Francisco Call, October 14, 1907, p. 7/2; cf. also A. E. Yoell, "The Oriental vs. American Labor," pp. 247-256. Even Governor Gillett's secretary recommended the League's facilities for information on Japanese exclusion from California's schools, cf. letter, David K. Pegues of Tennessee to Governor Gillett, March 25, 1909, Gillett Papers, GP7:92, California State Archives.

[43]San Francisco Call, May 13, 1907, p. 7/3. The League prepared pamphlets on the resolutions introduced in Congress. The legislation was circulated throughout the United States, San Francisco Call, April 21, 1907, p. 39/4.

[44]San Francisco Call, May 13, 1907, p. 7/3.

[45]San Francisco Call, May 22, 1911, p. 5/3. Yoell stated that statistics on Japanese exports compiled by the League were used in a monthly magazine in Milan, Italy. The A. E. L., Proceedings were sent to the members of the California Legislature and every central labor organization throughout California in 1913 to attempt to influence the legislature to pass an anti alien land bill, cf. A. E. L., Proceedings, March 16, 1913, p. 299.

The composition and statistical increases in the League's membership was another factor in its propaganda campaign. Throughout the eight years of its existence, the League's membership consisted primarily of union men and tended to increase through 1909. Perhaps one of the reasons for a decrease in membership was a corresponding decrease in immigration. With a decrease in Japanese immigration after 1908,[46] plus a number of other factors, the League would lose much power and influence by 1913. Yet, the League's resolutions on exclusion were also adopted by several other organizations, including:

> The Ancient Order of Foresters, Iroquois Club, California Council Daughters of Liberty, Holly Park Improvement Club, San Francisco Democratic Club, Sailors Union of the Pacific, International Association of Machinists, American Brotherhood of Cement Workers, International Association of Blacksmiths and Helpers, International Association of Electrical Workers, the Building Trades Council of California, the San Francisco Labor Council, plus 219 "organizations" and a large number of individual endorsements--all of which amounted to 877,500 citizens.[47]

Within four months of October 1905, the League "increased the number of organizations affiliated with the League to 174 as against 166 at the last [January 1906] meeting."[48] Yoell reported that five civic and seven fraternal organizations withdrew their membership leaving: eight civic organizations; twenty-four fraternal and benevolent organizations; one military organization; and 141 labor organizations--amounting to 1,100,000 citizens endorsing the League's resolutions.[49] At the Second Annual meeting of the League in May 1907, Yoell claimed there were 225 organizations affiliated with the League; 198 were labor unions--totaling 91,500 citizens.[50] The Fourth Annual Report in May 1909, shows the affiliated organizations amounted to 238, and a gain of only eight by the Fifth Annual Report.[51] The Sixth Annual Report states there were 272 organizations carrying the results of the League's efforts into all of the Pacific Coast States as well as into British Columbia, Idaho, Colorado, Montana, Nevada, and Nebraska.[52]

---

[46]The Report of the Commissioner General of Immigration, Table XV, "Immigration, fiscal years ended June 30, 1899 to 1915, by races or peoples," states that Japanese immigration increased 1905-1907: 11,021, 14,243, 30,824, and began to decline 1908-1911: 16,418, 3,275, 2,798, 4,575, p. 122. Cf. also Gillett Papers (especially GP7:103), California State Archives, and San Francisco Call, January 29, 1909, p. 2/7; San Francisco Call, February 12, 1909, p. 4/5.

[47]San Francisco Call, October 23, 1905, p. 12/1. All these figures were presented by A. E. Yoell, cf. also A. E. L., Proceedings, March 8, 1908, p. 1; op. cit., September 20, 1908, p. 3; op. cit., January 17, 1909, p. 3.

[48]San Francisco Call, February 5, 1906, p. 13/4.

[49]Ibid. Even though a few of the civic and fraternal organizations decided not to participate in the League's cause, it did not forget their initial interest. To maintain interest in the League's activities "a large number of delegates volunteered to give one night a week to the work of visiting civic, industrial, and fraternal organizations to present the purpose and accomplishments of the League," San Francisco Call, May 13, 1907, p. 7/3.

[50]San Francisco Examiner, May 13, 1907, p. 4/6; San Francisco Call, May 13, 1907, p. 7/3.

Not only did the League expand in membership, it tended to expand geographically outside of San Francisco. Within six months of its founding in May 1905, P. H. McCarthy addressed the members on "the necessity of establishing branch leagues throughout the State to co-operate with the League and help to raise the funds necessary to carry the [exclusion] bill to a successful end."[53] Most, if not all of these, "branch" leagues were affiliated with the State American Federation of Labor or State Building Trades Council.[54] The expansion of the League's efforts outside San Francisco was due to increased attention in the newspapers as well as propaganda printed by the League, especially after the San Francisco school segregation incident of 1906.[55]

It was not until 1907 that the League established "branches" outside California, locating them in Seattle, Anaconda, and Denver.[56] After May 1907, communications with the San Francisco League increased from Spokane and Seattle. A "mammoth" convention was even convened in Seattle to frame a Japanese exclusion law similar to the Chinese Exclusion Act.[57] The convention, originally planned for December 15, did not begin until February 3, 1908, at the Labor Temple, Seattle, Washington. The three day convention was attended by 132 delegates from California, Nevada,

---

[51] San Francisco Call, May 17, 1909, p. 5/4; A. E. L., Proceedings, May 15, 1910, p. 4.

[52] San Francisco Call, May 22, 1911, p. 5/3; A. E. L., Proceedings, May 21, 1911, p. 112. Of the 272 organizations, fourteen were outside San Francisco and seventeen were branch leagues outside California.

[53] San Francisco Call, November 27, 1905, p. 12/5.

[54] Branch leagues were located in Santa Clara County, Marin, Stockton, San Jose, Alameda, Vallejo, San Mateo, Fresno, and Sacramento; cf. San Francisco Call, May 13, 1907, p. 7/3; A. E. L., Proceedings, November 15, 1908, p. 9; San Francisco Call, October 6, 1908, p. 10/2; San Francisco Call, April 18, 1910, p. 5/5. Sacramento Union, October 9, 1910, p. 9/4. The Union reported that the A. E. L. of Sacramento was formed by members of the Federated Trades Council. The President of the League, George W. Metzgar, was a member of the Carpenter's Union.

[55] San Francisco Call, April 21, 1907, p. 39/4; San Francisco Call, October 14, 1907, p. 7/2.

[56] San Francisco Call, May 13, 1907, p. 7/3. F. W. Matson states "the Seattle Chapter was founded by A. E. Fowler, an ex-hotel clerk who formented large-scale riots in Washington and Vancouver during 1907. Shortly thereafter he was arrested, declared insane in a court hearing, and committed to the state asylum," op. cit., p. 10. Fowler seems to have found a more appreciative audience in San Francisco since the A. E. L., Proceedings lists him as a delegate for membership to the League's executive board on May 15, 1910, p. 18. Fowler later became the editor of an anti Japanese journal called The White Man, which was published in large editions at irregular intervals. During January 1911, Fowler sold large numbers of the magazine in Sacramento and Stockton. He accepted donations for sending large numbers of the magazine to various points in the East, with the object of influencing legislation in favor of Asiatic exclusion, San Francisco Call, March 7, 1911, p. 19/2; A. E. L., Proceedings, January 1910, p. 12.

[57] San Francisco Call, October 14, 1907, p. 7/2. The League in San Francisco planned on sending 500 delegates.

Colorado, Nebraska, Oregon,[58] Washington, and British Columbia.[59] Tveitmoe and Yoell were unanimously elected permanent Chairman and Secretary of the convention which was opened with a lengthy speech by C. O. Young, a "special" representative of the American Federation of Labor, who set the tone for the three-day convention.

> From San Francisco the present agitation has spread over the entire Pacific Coast to such an extent that there is a great deal of enmity and criticism throughout different localities, and some of the papers are knocking about undesirable citizens of the white race because they agitate against the brown and yellow man. We are not antagonistic to them because they are brown or yellow, but we are opposed to the breaking down of the conditions that the white races have built ... wherever those people have touched a country its conditions have been changed and its standard of living lowered. We are loyal to the flag that floats over our country, an emblem of liberty, and I never want to see the time when that flag has a yellow streak in it. I do not want to see the time when citizenship must be accorded to a people whose morals, whose standard of living, whose customs of life, are not in accordance with our customs, standards of living and civilization.[60]

Some twenty or thirty speeches of this nature were given by members of the delegation. On the final day of the convention, C. O. Young was elected President of the Asiatic Exclusion League of North America. When a dispute arose over who was to be elected Secretary-Treasurer, Young resigned from the office and Tveitmoe and Yoell were elected as President and Secretary against their objections. In fact, the delegates from San Francisco carried nearly all the offices.

It would seem that the convention ended in failure primarily because Tveitmoe and Yoell could not effectively handle an organization spread over six states and British Columbia.[61] However, three months later, the annual report by A. E. Yoell

---

[58] The opposition to Japanese was not restricted to labor unions. There were other factors working to create an anti Japanese stereotype. The San Francisco Call reports that a play entitled "The Jap" was first shown in Portland, Oregon, and created a favorable impression. "The story is one of intrigue involving a plot to smuggle Japanese into the country, the surrender of plans of the fortification on Puget Sound to the Mikado's gover-ment and an interesting love story. The hero is 'The Jap,' who is connected with the embassy at Washington, D.C. The play was well received," San Francisco Call, February 9, 1909, p. 2/3.

[59] A. E. L., Proceedings of the First International Convention of the Asiatic Exclusion League of North America, pp. 1; 16. The delegates from California were from Eureka, Los Angeles, Oakland, and mostly San Francisco. The delegates from San Francisco included Frank McGowan, E. C. Loomis, Charles F. Knight, J. B. Bowen, and Andrew Furuseth, cf. p. 17.

[60] Ibid., p. 6.

[61] The date of Monday, March 4, 1909, was set for the second meeting of the International Convention in Vancouver. The A. E. L., Proceedings in April 1909, make no mention of a meeting in Vancouver.

claimed branch leagues "were established in practically all of the important cities on the Pacific Coast by the parent organization in this city."[62]

Since the Exclusion League of San Francisco did not effectively expand outside California, what was probably being referred to was a newly established Anti-Japanese Laundry League, formed in March 1908, by the laundry proprietors and employees in San Francisco. Their intent was to prevent the issuance of licenses to Japanese, reduce their patronage, and to prevent them from securing laundry equipment.[63] The President of the Laundry League, H. F. McMahon, and the Secretary, R. C. Hurst, were members of, and delegates to, the Asiatic Exclusion League.[64] By November, the Laundry League maintained branches in Alameda, Stockton, Vallejo, and San Mateo.[65] A mass meeting was held in San Mateo on November 22, 1908, and was attended by delegates from the Asiatic Exclusion Leagues of San Francisco, Oakland, San Mateo, and Santa Clara counties for the purpose of discussing the objectives of the laundry association. "Practically every laundry owner and operator on the peninsula and the Santa Clara Valley was represented at the meeting in addition to a large number of employees who were urged to attend the conference."[66] The Laundry League was also successful in establishing branches in Sacramento, Reno, and Fresno.

---

[62]<u>San Francisco Call</u>, May 11, 1908, p. 7/5. P. H. McCarthy reported that on his eastern trip he found that "the workmen of the Atlantic seaboard have become radically anti-Japanese." Even as late as 1911, the League claimed influence in "all of the Pacific Coast states as well as British Columbia, Idaho, Colorado, Montana, Nevada, and Nebraska," <u>San Francisco Call</u>, May 23, 1911, p. 5/3.

[63]R. L. Buell, "The Development of Anti-Japanese Agitation in the United States, II," <u>Political Science Quarterly</u>, 38 (1923), p. 59. Since Japanese were not citizens, they could not join the white unions. Japanese therefore formed their own laundry union in San Francisco, Oakland, and Alameda. <u>San Francisco Call</u>, June 15, 1907, p. 4/6.

[64]A. E. L., <u>Proceedings</u>, November 15, 1908, p. 9, and December 20, 1908, p. 5. Cf. also Kessler, <u>op. cit.</u>, p. 73, note 19; Matson, <u>op. cit.</u>, p. 10. Matson maintains that "within a year, the league had established locals in San Mateo, San Rafael, Fresno, and Oakland," p. 11. Other citations of agitation by McMahon and Hurst can be found in <u>San Francisco Call</u>, February 9, 1909, p. 2/3; <u>San Francisco Call</u>, January 5, 1911, p. 12/2. Hurst, in 1911, reported that the board of health had ordered the Japanese and Chinese owners in San Francisco to place their laundries in sanitary conditions.

[65]A. E. L., <u>Proceedings</u>, November 15, 1908, p. 9. I. B. Cross maintains that "attempts to form similar leagues in other communities were not successful," Cross, <u>op. cit.</u>, p. 265.

[66]<u>San Francisco Call</u>, November 22, 1908, p. 22/2. On December 6, 1908, a State Convention of the Anti-Jap Laundry League was held at 222 Van Ness Avenue. The speakers were Tveitmoe, Benham, Casey, and R. A. A. Summers, A. E. L., <u>Proceedings</u>, December 20, 1908, p. 5. Some of what was discussed at the November and December meetings will be found in A. E. Yoell, "Oriental vs. American Labor," p. 250.

The Laundry League at Sacramento was organized by Joseph Chironi, W. Warner, and Harry Dubecker. In a letter to the San Francisco league, Dubecker reported that

> In our city, on L Street from Second to Fourth Street, you will find nothing but Japanese, and in such numbers that it is certainly alarming. On the corner of 4th and L streets a small merchandise store was started some three years ago on a very small scale; today it has developed into a very large concern and doing an extensive business. Our berry and fruit industry in this valley is controlled entirely by Japs. The very sight of the thousands of these coolies in our midst is enough to arouse any patriotic American citizen. I know that I shall do all in my power to help remove this menace to a different atmosphere than our own American soil.[67]

The League's branches in Reno and Fresno seemed to have used more forceful measures than dissent and mass meetings.[68] The secretary of the Reno League reported that the Nevada Steam Laundry, owned by Japanese, had been closed because of lack of patronage.[69] It was not until early in 1912 that the Laundry League established a branch in Fresno. To discourage patronage of Oriental washhouses, League members were asking white people to place their names on a list entitled, "We don't patronize Japs." Such a technique of discrimination was reported to be "making good headway."[70] Such acts of open discrimination and organized opposition to the Japanese in the laundry business was only a small part of the effect to exclude Japanese from American society.[71]

---

[67] A. E. L., Pacific Coast Convention of the Anti-Jap Laundry League, San Francisco, May 9, 1909, pp. 10-11.

[68] McMahon, in March 1910, stated that there had not been any new Japanese laundries started "since the formation of the white men's order." He also hoped to convince the Emporium, among other business houses, that its employment of Japanese should not be continued, San Francisco Call, March 21, 1910, p. 5/1.

[69] San Francisco Call, August 9, 1910, p. 4/6.

[70] San Francisco Call, February 18, 1912, p. 68/4. Billboard advertisements were also used. One read: "Foolish woman! Spending your man's earnings on Japs. Be fair, patronize your own. We support you," R. L. Buell, "The Development of Anti-Japanese Agitation in the United States, II," p. 59.

[71] There were 107 Japanese laundries employing 1,005 Japanese in the State of California by 1913, cf. Report of the Bureau of Labor Statistics, "Japanese Statistics," p. 622, Appendix to the Journal of the Senate and Assembly of the Fortieth Session of the Legislature, III, 1913. These figures should be compared to statements of A. E. Yoell who claimed that the Japanese reduced the white union laundry workers in San Francisco from 1,650 in 1905, to 1,050 by 1909. The Japanese had sixteen businesses employing 276 people in San Francisco by 1913, cf. A. E. Yoell, "Oriental vs. American Labor," p. 250; Report of the Bureau of Labor Statistics, op. cit., p. 615; and San Francisco Call, April 24, 1911, p. 6/7.

The Asiatic Exclusion League, in its first four years, enjoyed success in nearly all of its endeavors as it extended in membership and locale. While new leagues and union interest increased, the League delegates continued to present anti-Japanese resolutions at the labor meetings.[72] But this was not enough for those League members who wanted action and results. The ultimate failure of the League seems to have been tied to two factors: the character and motivation of the League's President, O. A. Tveitmoe, and the involvement of the League in political controversies. On a number of occasions the League was forced to reverse and contradict its established policies which caused confusion not only within the League, but to the general public, and especially to the politicians.

---

[72]Andrew J. Gallagher, President of the San Francisco Labor Council, acted as the A. E. L. delegate to the National Convention of the American Federation of Labor. He introduced resolutions into the executive committee to extend the exclusion act to include all classes of Asiatics, San Francisco Call, February 2, 1910, p. 7/2; San Francisco Call, February 8, 1913, p. 8/7. In December 1909 the Building Trades Council, on the national level, printed 75,000 copies of resolutions passed at their Tampa, Florida, convention. These pamphlets were sent to Congress and the affiliated organizations of the A. E. L., San Francisco Call, December 3, 1909, p. 5/7.

CHAPTER III

THE STORMY PETREL OF LABOR CIRCLES:
THE LEAGUE AND POLITICS, 1905-1913

His [Olaf A. Tveitmoe's] muttered answer was the 'first, I am going to kill that Golden Rule fellow,' [Lincoln Stephens] ... 'But, Tveit,' said Anton Johannsen, 'I thought you were going to kill the Golden Rule.' 'No,' Tveitmoe bumbled in his chest, 'I would not kill that fellow. He's all right. He ain't got no pope.' And it appeared that what had won him was that I had not quoted Marx or any other authority, but had appealed to reason, his and mine .... Tveitmoe was a trusting friend of mine the rest of his life. He would let me into the most sacred of labor confidence in every emergency.

    Lincoln Stephens, The Autobiography of Lincoln Stephens,
       pp. 690-691.

Behind him [Patrick H. McCarthy] was a master-mind in the person of another laborite, O. A. Tveitmoe, a dark Scandinavian of powerful build, a 'gorilla,' who was Secretary of the Building Trades Council, boss of the Labor Party, and Sam Gomper's big friend and trusted henchman on the coast.

    Louis Adamic, Dynamite, pp. 201-202.

CHAPTER III

THE STORMY PETREL OF LABOR CIRCLES:
THE LEAGUE AND POLITICS, 1905-1913

It seems that the League was destined to become involved in politics from the day it was founded. The Mayor of San Francisco, Eugene Schmitz, gave a speech at the first formal meeting of the League.[1] He was among the honored speakers at the mass anti-Japanese rally in December 1906,[2] and he was the guest of honor at the State Building Trades Council Convention at San Jose.[3]

What is ironic and confusing about these events is the fact that two years before the Exclusion League was formed, Tveitmoe was outspokenly opposed to the Union Labor Party--referring to its leaders and members as a bunch of

> prattling parasites who preach class hatred and scare away investors from this great and glorious city .... An individual, whether his name be Schmitz or Ruef, who by his official acts and personal ambition for private gain, drives capital away from San Francisco and steals our chances of employment.[4]

It seems fairly certain that by 1906, Tveitmoe himself was looking for personal political gain, and the Exclusion League was to help catapult him into political office shortly after the San Francisco earthquake.

It was this earthshaking event which also precipitated the well known controversy between the San Francisco school board, Mayor Eugene Schmitz, and President Roosevelt over the exclusion and segregation of Japanese students from the city's public schools.[5] At first, the Exclusion League had no intention of becoming

---

[1]San Francisco Call, May 8, 1905, p. 2/1.

[2]San Francisco Examiner, December 24, 1906, p. 1/1. Schmitz declared that "corporations and trusts favor the admission of the Japanese as a move to disrupt labor organizations in this country," San Francisco Call, December 24, 1906, p. 2/2.

[3]San Francisco Call, January 10, 1906, p. 7/1.

[4]E. J. Rowell, The Union Labor Party of San Francisco, 1901-1911, p. 82. Cf. San Francisco Call, November 1, 1903. Rowell states that McCarthy and Tveitmoe opposed, and later supported, the Union Labor Party for "personal political expediency apart from the development within his own [Building Trades Council] unions," p. 123.

[5]The best accounts of this event can be found in Bailey, Roosevelt and the Japanese-American Crisis, and Esthus, Theodore Roosevelt and Japan. The latter book includes material from the Japanese side of the controversy. The Secretary of Commerce and Labor, Victor H. Metcalf, reported there were ninety-three Japanese pupils in twenty-three public schools in San Francisco, cf. Walton Bean, California, An Interpretive History, p. 332.

involved in the question. Andrew Furuseth pointed out that the League would receive "scant courtesy" at the state legislature since the President had strongly requested that the State exercise moderation in dealing with the Japanese question. "Furuseth said it would be better for the cause not to suffer defeat before the State Legislature, for such loss would hurt the movement in the Eastern States."[6] Tveitmoe rhetorically agreed: "What is the use of going up to Sacramento when we know beforehand that we will not be favorably received?"[7]

A week later, Tveitmoe launched the League into the middle of the school controversy. While the conference between Mayor Schmitz, the school board, and the President was taking place, Tveitmoe wired Schmitz not to desert the laboring man.

> If President wants to humiliate the American flag, let him tell California's Governor and Legislature to repeal the law, but he cannot coerce free Californians to bow in submission to the will of the Mikado. Roosevelt's power will not make one white man out of all the Japs in the Nipponese Empire. California is the white man's country, and not the Caucasian graveyard.[8]

Four days later, Tveitmoe visited Sacramento for a conference with members of the state legislature "to learn the exact status of the bills and resolutions affecting the Japanese question now pending before the legislature."[9] Tveitmoe predicted that Senator Keane's amendment to the school bill, plus a number of other bills and resolutions would be passed by the legislature. He sent off another telegram to Mayor Schmitz which stated:

> The exclusion laws must not be dependent upon the changing opinions of the Nation's executive. Extend the provisions of the Chinese exclusion laws by act of Congress to Japanese and Koreans, and enforce it amicably and rigidly. This is the only solution of the problem.[10]

---

[6]San Francisco Call, February 3, 1907, p. 24/4. On another occasion there was agitation in the public schools of Sausalito against some Korean students. When a resolution was proposed to commend the action of the Sausalito trustees and extend them the support of the League, the matter was considered out of the jurisdiction of the League and the resolution was tabled and the question referred to the executive committee, San Francisco Call, March 9, 1908, p. 5/4.

[7]San Francisco Call, February 3, 1907, p. 24/4.

[8]San Francisco Call, February 11, 1907, cited in Buell, "The Development of Anti-Japanese Agitation in the United States, I," p. 630. Schmitz later reported to Tveitmoe that "during the conference on February 10, the President exhibited the greatest rage, demanding of Schmitz: 'who is this man who dares insult the President of the United States?' He pounded the mahogany with his gavel and nearly hit the ceiling in his anger," San Francisco Call, March 11, 1907, p. 1/3.

[9]San Francisco Call, February 15, 1907, p. 5/4.

[10]Ibid. Ira E. Bennett, the San Francisco Call correspondent in Washington stated: "It is pretty safe to predict that Japanese exclusion is in sight," ibid.

When Roosevelt proposed a compromise on the issue by granting "exclusion" if the state would allow Japanese students back into the schools, Tveitmoe thought the Mayor had made a satisfactory agreement with the President. "In fact, I think the Mayor has obtained more concessions from the President than the President has gotten from the Mayor."[11] As he congratulated Schmitz, Tveitmoe scapegoated the President.

> The race question is the big thing. The school question is only an incident. If we had received a real exclusion law in return for the concessions in the matter of the schools, the bargain would not have been so bad, but the arrangement made is, in my opinion, about as sour lemon as the President could have handed the Pacific Coast. Of course, we are given to understand that something more is promised us; if we are very, very good. Whether that something more is another large-sized lemon, 'the soft word,' a gold brick, or a big stick, remains to be seen.[12]

At the following monthly meeting of the Executive Committee of the Exclusion League, Tveitmoe pointed out that the actions of the Mayor and the School Board had been hastily and unjustly criticized and that the Mayor's actions "when it is understood--will be recognized as one of the greatest achievements of statesmanship of the age."[13] It was evident to the Call reporter that a big change had come over many of the members who had previously expressed themselves freely and vigorously in denouncing the Mayor. On the following day, the Executive Committee met with the exclusion delegates and adopted two resolutions: one introduced by Walter Macarthur was to continue agitation for the enactment of a Japanese exclusion law, and the other, introduced by P. H. McCarthy, was to thank Schmitz and the Board of Education for their work in Washington. A dispute arose among the delegates when McCarthy proposed to refer his resolution to the Executive Committee for an investigation as to whether or not a note of thanks was due Schmitz and the board. On a tie vote, Tveitmoe declared McCarthy's resolution lost and the delegates passed the resolution to thank the Mayor. Many of the delegates complained that politics had been introduced in the meeting and many others left the hall, weary of the long debate.[14]

The most likely reason for this high praise of the Mayor was Tveitmoe's appointment to San Francisco's Board of Supervisors when it was found that three supervisors had accepted bribes for the defeat of an ordinance designed to regulate

---

[11]San Francisco Call, February 17, 1907, p. 39/2. Tveitmoe was confident that an exclusion law would be passed by Congress and "that it will be due largely to the efforts of Mayor Schmitz."

[12]San Francisco Call, February 20, 1907, p. 3/1-2.

[13]San Francisco Call, March 10, 1907, p. 33/2. Cf. also San Francisco Call, March 7, 1907, p. 3/6.

[14]San Francisco Call, March 11, 1907, p. 1/3 and p. 2/6.

the operation of skating rinks.[15] With the removal of Schmitz from office, Tveitmoe used his position as supervisor to oppose and boycott Mayor Edward Taylor because "he is a lawyer and has been concerned most of his life with vested interests where his sympathies would naturally incline. I do not think he is a man of the masses."[16]

Tveitmoe's apparent successes at this time, in both labor and political circles, led him to consider running for the office of Mayor.[17] It was not long until Tveitmoe's dark past caught up with him.[18] On September 24, 1907, the Evening Bulletin published a front page article relating how Tveitmoe purchased the Crookston Tribune in Crookston, Minnesota in 1892, by forging a $200 note. He had been tried and convicted and on April 16, he was sentenced to serve eighteen months in Stillwater. He reached the prison on April 20 and served until December 21, when he was pardoned by Governor Nelson of Minnesota.[19]

---

[15] Rowell, op. cit., p. 163. J. J. O'Neill of the Typographical Union, an Exclusion League delegate, was appointed along with Tveitmoe. Rowell also states that O'Neill and Tveitmoe "were without complicity in regard to the charges of corruption," p. 148. F. L. Ryan, Industrial Relations in the San Francisco Building Trades, p. 33, note 29, states that Tveitmoe was appointed a supervisor by Schmitz in 1906. Cf. also San Francisco Call, January 12, 1907, p. 3/3.

[16] San Francisco Call, July 17, 1907, p. 3/1; San Francisco Call, August 6, 1907, p. 14/3; San Francisco Call, August 8, 1907, p. 1/5; San Francisco Call, August 12, 1907, p. 2/2; San Francisco Call, August 28, 1907, p. 5/2. When the Supreme Court removed all doubt as to the legality of Taylor's election and appointment of a new board, Tveitmoe ceased his boycott of supervisor's meetings.

[17] Tveitmoe was the secretary of the general strike committee of the 25 Carmen's Union which struck in July costing the city and labor millions of dollars. San Francisco Call, July 13, 1907, p. 7/6; San Francisco Call, July 24, 1907, p. 4/6. The San Francisco Call reported that "Tveitmoe does not say, 'I want it,' [the Mayor's job] but remarks diplomatically, 'If I should be nominated, I would consider it my duty to accept,'" San Francisco Call, August 17, 1907, p. 2/3.

[18] Edward J. Livernash, editor of the Bulletin, carried on an intense battle against Tveitmoe's rise to political office, San Francisco Call, August 12, 1907, p. 2/2. Upon the publication of the exposé article, Tveitmoe retorted: "I knew that Edward J. Livernash has been preparing something against me, but they've gone too far," San Francisco Call, September 25, 1907, p. 2/2.

[19] The Evening Bulletin published a large photo showing Tveitmoe in prison garb, a shaved head, and the Stillwater convict number 3920 on his chest. On pages 3-5 is a complete transcript of the judgment roll. Tveitmoe's response was, "I don't know where they got all that stuff, or whether it is made up or is the record of some other man possible with the same name, but it isn't me. I can't see any likeness in these pictures, can you?," San Francisco Call, September 25, 1907, p. 2/2.

To all of this, Tveitmoe entered a full denial:

> It is a lie from start to finish; I was never charged with the crime of forgery; I was never tried on such a charge; I never was convicted of any crime; I never served time in the Minnesota State Prison, and I never was pardoned by Governor Nelson .... The boys are all with me, they were a bit mad at first and wanted to go down tonight and blow up the Bulletin office, but I stopped them and told them tomorrow would be plenty of time to act.[20]

Tveitmoe threatened to bring a civil suit for a million dollars against the Bulletin for such a political attack on his character. He claimed that he had not been a candidate for Mayor and had been "seriously considering withdrawing from public life, but now--I may decide to be a candidate for Mayor after all."[21] But Tveitmoe neither brought suit nor did he run for Mayor, for the evidence was too well documented to be false.[22]

Referred to as an "impenitent convict," an unsuccessful minority tried to remove Tveitmoe and McCarthy from control of the Building Trades Council.[23] The revelation of Tveitmoe's character brought distrust and apprehension from the police department on the League's motives. Rumors began to circulate that the League was backing a movement to start a riot in San Francisco with the arrival of the Great White Fleet, sent around the world by Roosevelt in 1908.[24] The members were shocked to find that the Chief of Police took some stock in the "wild tale," so the delegates asked San Francisco judge James G. Maguire to defend the League's purposes.

> The assaults upon this and kindred organizations of this coast are similar to the attacks upon every movement destined to elevate the masses. . am here to contradict any suspicion of anarchy which might be cast upon this league. I believe in the universal brotherhood and equality of man, but I see no inconsistency in keeping our country for ourselves. I believe that all men are created equal, but that is no reason why I should open the door of my house to everyone who wants to enter. Assimilation is impossible. If Japan desires to extend her civilization, we have nothing to gain. Will

---

[20]Ibid. Such a statement should be kept in mind since Tveitmoe was deeply involved with the bombings of the Los Angeles Times in 1910.

[21]Ibid.

[22]San Francisco Call, December 31, 1911, p. 18/2; F. L. Ryan, op. cit., p. 32, note 29.

[23]San Francisco Call, November 25, 1907, p. 2/1. Tveitmoe seems to have used the columns of the Building Trades journal, Organized Labor, as a pulpit against his enemies. He had charged former union Secretary with attempting to destroy the Building Trades Council a few years before Tveitmoe took over. The irate Secretary attacked Tveitmoe on the street with a brick, San Francisco Call, April 16, 1907, p. 14/2.

[24]San Francisco Call, March 29, 1908, p. 38/7.

you consent to lose your own standard, which is the evidence of
your work in the cause of civilization? It is not necessary to
decide whether we or the Asiatics are the superior race. We
cannot change our cattle pasture into a sheep range.

Having suffered setbacks in local politics and frustrations of the League's goals in Congress,[26] certain members of the League began to agitate for discriminatory legislation against Japanese in the California State Legislature. Senator Marc Anthony, the League's most outspoken representative in the State Legislature, and ex-Senator Frank McGowan made speeches "advocating the pledging of legislative candidates to the support of the principles of the League."[27] As early as July 1907, Tveitmoe "instructed the executive committee to communicate with the platform committees of the national political parties and get them to place the parties on record in the Japanese exclusion matter."[28] Formal resolutions were drawn up and ordered sent to the Republican and Democratic National Conventions with the request that they be inserted in their platforms in June 1908.[29] Congressman Julius Kahn reported to the delegates

> The reason no action has been taken is because the majority of
> the representatives from eastern states do not realize conditions. It is not a question of politics, but a question of
> educating the eastern people as to the existing conditions.
> Both political parties will be in favor of Asiatic exclusion
> when they understand, more fully, what the residents of the
> Pacific Coast have to deal with. I feel confident that a law
> will be passed, an exclusion law which will be satisfactory
> to the people of the Pacific Coast.[30]

When the Democratic platform was formalized, it contained a plank favoring the exclusion of Asiatic laborers from the United States which caused some Japanese to express indignation. The majority of the Democrats evaded the issue by implying that the plank was not anti-Japanese, but was incorporated in the platform for the purpose of satisfying the labor element.[31] There were certain Democrats, however, who were determined to ally the Exclusion League to the Democratic Party since the Republicans were silent on the exclusion issue. Andrew Furuseth and

---

[25]San Francisco Call, April 13, 1908, p. 4/3. Maguire was evidently looking for votes since he was the Democratic candidate for Congress from the fourth district, San Francisco Call, October 26, 1908, p. 1/1.

[26]Speakers reported to the League delegates that "more than 1,000 petitions sent to Congress by citizens of the coast protesting against the Japanese had been misplaced," San Francisco Call, March 9, 1908, p. 5/4.

[27]San Francisco Call, May 11, 1908, p. 7/5. Although there were anti-Japanese and anti-Asiatic bills in the State Legislature in 1907, the League was more concerned with the national issue of the school exclusion and obtaining a Congressional bill extending Chinese exclusion to the Japanese.

[28]San Francisco Call, July 15, 1907, p. 11/1.

[29]San Francisco Call, June 15, 1908, p. 9/5.

[30]Ibid.

[31]San Francisco Call, July 13, 1908, p. 1/3.

State Senator Anthony Caminetti attempted to pass a resolution "that the Asiatic Exclusion League urge upon the people of this coast and elsewhere to vote in this election for the Democratic nominee."[32] This meeting was attended by nearly 1,000 delegates who listened to Caminetti's fierce tirade against the Republican administration, while Furuseth read speeches by Bryan on the subject. It is noteworthy to state that Tveitmoe did not rule Caminetti out of order since it was contrary to the constitution of the League, which was supposed to be strictly non-partisan.[33] The controversy lasted for four hours and forty minutes with a vote of ninety-eight to fourteen to refuse endorsement of W. J. Bryan and the congressional candidates of the Democratic Party.[34]

Even without the backing of the Exclusion League, the Democratic Party circulated anti-Asiatic pamphlets in California. They stated in bold caption, "The success of Mr. Bryan and the Democratic Party will serve notice on the world that this continent shall be preserved for our own people, for American institutions, and for Western Civilization."[35]

Although the Democrats lost the national election in 1908, certain Democrats pursued an anti-Japanese campaign in the California Legislature--perhaps partly for recognition in the newspaper--but most certainly as a means of causing embarrassment to the Republican administration in Washington, D.C. The Exclusion League took a much more active interest in the politicians after 1908. State Senator Marc Anthony actively sought the backing of the Exclusion League by attending their meetings.

> To the cordial introduction of your presiding officer, [Tveitmoe] my response is that at the approaching session of the State Legislature I shall do exactly what each of you would do in my place--work soberly, devotedly and wholly for the best interests

---

[32]San Francisco Call, October 19, 1908. p. 7/5.

[33]Ibid. Tveitmoe was noted for ruling the League's speakers with an iron hand. When one of the delegates proposed a boycott as the best means to be pursued to hamper the Japanese in their various enterprises, Tveitmoe thundered: "I will have none of that. This is an exclusion league, not an institution for the furtherance of boycotts. We will have none of that discussion here," San Francisco Call, February 4, 1907, p. 2/5; and San Francisco Call, May 17, 1909, p. 5/4.

[34]San Francisco Call, October 26, 1908, p. 1/1. The Secretary of the San Francisco Labor Council, Andrew J. Gallagher, introduced a resolution to repudiate the movement to take away the league's non-partisan character. The concept was originally taken from the constitution of the American Federation of Labor, cf. San Francisco Call, September 13, 1908, p. 20/3.

[35]Democratic Campaign Pamphlet, Scrapbook, Phelan Collection, pp. 64-65, cited in Kessler, The Political Factors in California Anti Alien Land Legislation, 1912-1913, p. 113. The finance committee for the Democratic Party was under the control of J. D. Phelan, while the executive committee was under the Chairmanship of J. B. Sanford of Ukiah. Both these men were outspoken anti-Japanese legislators, San Francisco Call, September 13, 1908, p. 20/3.

of the people of the State of California and for the exclusion of Asiatics. As an honorary member of your magnificent organization, I esteem it an eviable privilege to be one of your representatives on the floor of the State Senate.[36]

In the 1909 State Legislature anti-Japanese bills were introduced by A. M. Drew, Grove Johnson, J. B. Sanford, and Marc Anthony.[37] Senate Bill 492 by Anthony was a measure to give the people of California an opportunity to express themselves at the polls on the Japanese question. The bill was forced to a vote and was defeated 22 to 12.[38] The League's representatives were irate over the defeat of the Anthony bill. The League took on the attributes of an inquisition when three Senators: E. J. Wolfe, I. J. Kennedy, and J. P. Hare, were asked to explain why they failed to vote on the Anthony bill. All three Senators "pledged themselves to work with the League in the future."[39] The League actively participated in agitating for state legislation against Japanese,[40] but little of it had any effect due to the fact that the President, the Governor, and the Speaker of the Assembly, Phil Stanton, were determined to stop the discriminatory legislation.[41]

With these political defeats in the legislature, the League became even more determined to pass legislation on the State level. A resolution, introduced by Charles F. Knight, stated:

---

[36] A. E. L., Proceedings, December 20, 1908, p. 24.

[37] Franklin Hichborn, Story of the Sessions of the California Legislature of 1909, p. 201, hereafter cited as Hichborn, Legislation of 1909. In all, the 1909 legislature discussed seventeen measures directed at the Japanese. Cf. Matson, The Anti-Japanese Movement in California: 1890-1942, p. 13. Another author claims there were five discriminatory measures introduced, cf. S. C. Olin, California's Prodigal Sons, p. 84.

[38] Hichborn, Legislation of 1909, pp. 214-215. Anthony obviously obtained his idea for this bill from John Keane, a State Legislator from San Francisco. During the 1907 legislative session, Keane introduced a bill to submit the question of Japanese exclusion to the people. "The poll on the question is merely meant to serve as a directory of sentiment for the guidance of Congress in dealing with the future," San Francisco Call, March 9, 1907, p. 2/4. It was not until November 1920, that the people of California expressed themselves on the Japanese question by making modifications on the 1913 Alien Land Law.

[39] San Francisco Call, March 21, 1910, p. 5/1. Yoell reported that five congressmen and one senator had pledged themselves to support all legislation that would tend toward the exclusion of all Asiatics, cf. A. E. L., Proceedings, March 20, 1910, pp. 13-14.

[40] San Francisco Call, January 29, 1909, p. 4/4; January 30, p. 7/5; February 7, p. 20/2.

[41] San Francisco Call, February 9, 1909, p. 1/2. Stanton purportedly broke the joint rules of the legislature when he utilized the pocket veto on a joint resolution introduced by Lester Burnett of San Francisco, calling upon Congress to extend the provisions of the Chinese Exclusion Act to all Asiatics, including the Japanese, San Francisco Call, March 8, 1909, p. 2/3.

that the Secretary of the League [A. E. Yoell] be and is hereby
instructed immediately to notify the officials of all political
parties, all clubs or other organizations and the public, through
the press, that if any person who thus violated his pledge is
nominated or endorsed for any public office or position that this
League proposes vigorously to oppose his election or appointment
to any public position.[42]

There were two major elections in California before the passage of the Alien Land Law in May 1913. The election of Governor and State legislators in 1910 and the complex Presidential election of 1912. Between these two elections the League was to lose its political power and its social prestige.

The League seemed determined to involve itself with election politics and candidates for office.[43] Theodore A. Bell, the Democratic candidate for Governor in 1910 was an ally of the San Francisco Exclusion League.[44] In March, Bell and Charles F. Curry, the Republican candidate for Governor, answered the League's invitation to express their ideas concerning Asiatic exclusion. Bell stated that the State of California had no power to enact an exclusion law but could enact laws to preserve public morals, health and safety. He alluded to Roosevelt's "big stick" control over the Japanese school issue:

> I believe California or any other state has the undoubted
> right in the exercise of her public powers, to segregate the
> children in her public schools in any manner that she may
> choose, and any attempted restraint upon this right by the
> federal government is a clear violation of her sovereignty as
> a state.[45]

---

[42] San Francisco Call, May 17, 1909, p. 5/4. Of the twenty-seven legislators from San Francisco, Senator Lester Burnett, D. J. Reily, and Assemblymen C. A. Nelson, N. N. Beatty were the only lawmakers to accept an invitation to attend the League meeting, cf. A. E. L., Proceedings, March 20, 1910, p. 15.

[43] There even seems to be some evidence that there was a tradition for California politicians to state their position on Oriental exclusion. The San Francisco City Attorney, Franklin K. Lane ran for the gubernatorial election of 1902. "Lane had for a campaign slogan the phrase, 'Lane's the man.' It developed, however, that he had a Chinese servant and to capitalize on the anti-Asiatic prejudices of the workers this was modified by the Schmitz adherents to become, 'Ah Chews the Man,'" cf. E. J. Rowell, op. cit., p. 78. During the Alien Land issue of 1913, Lane (as Wilson's Secretary of the Interior) told the President that California would pass discriminating legislation, cf. P. E. Coletta, "The Most Thankless Task," p. 165. Even before Gillett became Governor, the San Francisco Call reported, "that congressmen Gillett had announced squarely that he was in favor of applying the Chinese Exclusion Law to the Japanese and Koreans." San Francisco Call, October 23, 1905, p. 12/1.

[44] A. E. L., Proceedings, May 1912, p. 221; Bell to W. J. Bryan, May 18, 1913, State Department Papers, 811.52/118, cited in Kessler, op. cit., p. 52, note 38. Bell assisted the League leaders in drafting an Asiatic Exclusion Law, cf. San Francisco Call, June 19, 1911, p. 12/6.

[45] San Francisco Call, March 21, 1910, p. 5/1.

Curry based his speech on the racial survival concept.

> It took our branch of the human race thousands of years to develop into our present stage of civilization ... it is essential that the blood of the American-European of this country who, together with their ancestors' developed civilization to its present state, should be kept pure and free from the taint of the decadent orientation of China, Japan, and India. We have no quarrel with those people. We wish them well in their own countries, but we do not want them in ours.[46]

Yoell explained that invitation had been sent to Alden Anderson, Hiram Johnson, and Philip A. Stanton, but no reply had been received.[47] Another candidate for Governor on the Republican ticket was Hiram Warren Johnson who avoided any contact with the League except for writing two letters on May 18 and July 29, 1910. In both letters Johnson turned down offers to be present and address the League. In both, however, he stated, "I favor Asiatic Exclusion."[48]

The following month, a committee of eleven members of the League was appointed to "canvass every section of the State and interview every candidate before the primaries in August."[49] The committee's president was A. C. Rose; its vice president, T. G. Negrich; and its secretary was A. E. Yoell who pointed out that a number of candidates in the previous election had not kept their pledges with the League, so steps were being taken to oppose the election of anyone who had violated his pledge.[50] The committee leveled their guns at the following candidates: Dominic J. Beban, Senatorial candidate from the twenty-fourth district; Nathan C. Coglan, Assemblyman from the forty-first district; George M. Perrine, Senatorial candidate from the twenty-fourth district; and Milton L. Schmitt, Assemblyman from the fortieth district.[51] They were repudiated for "clubbing with the 'big stick,' the 'patronage act,' the 'veto club,' and the trained ring masters of politics, betraying

---

[46] Charles Forrest Curry, Secretary of State before the 1910 elections, easily won the primary votes of Republicans in San Francisco and Sacramento counties, but Hiram Johnson carried the State with almost more votes than all the other candidates combined, S. C. Olin, op. cit., p. 29.

[47] A. E. L., Proceedings, April 17, 1910, p. 10, contains a letter from Alden Anderson in which he points out that he was present and participated in the founding of the League in May 1905, and had not changed his views on exclusion. Anderson was the State Superintendent of Banks, cf. Olin, op. cit., p. 24. Stanton also submitted a letter expressing his views on the immigration issue and that the League knew where he stood--therefore, "he did not see that it was necessary to appear at the meeting," San Francisco Call, April 18, 1910, p. 5/5.

[48] A. E. L., Proceedings, September 18, 1910, p. 55. The letters may be found in Johnson Papers, Bancroft Library, cf. S. C. Olin, op. cit., p. 210, note 42. J. B. Kessler points out that Johnson "identified the League as an appendage of the Southern Pacific machine which had opposed him in the 1910 Republican primary and in the general election of that year," cf. Johnson to McLaughlin, May 21, 1913, Johnson Papers, cited in Kessler, op. cit., p. 71.

[49] San Francisco Call, April 18, 1910, p. 5/5.

[50] San Francisco Call, May 28, 1910, p. 5/4.

[51] Ibid.; A. E. L., Proceedings, June 19, 1910, pp. 23-24; San Francisco Call, August 9, 1910, p. 4/5.

California and voting for the Japs."[52] The League may be charged with "playing politics" since all of these candidates were Republicans and it could hardly expect to win much favor with the election of a Progressive-Republican Governor.[53]

The presidential election of 1912, like the governor's campaign of 1910, again involved the League in political campaign issues. Before the election of November 5, 1912, the League circulated a questionnaire soliciting the endorsement of the League's program. Twenty-one of the state's forty Senate seats were contested in the 1912 election and of these, nine of the victors "were committed to the League's legislative program."[54] Of the eighty contested seats in the State Assembly, only twenty-eight successful candidates of the Republican and Democratic parties responded to the questionnaire. These districts all were situated in Northern or Central California.[55] Kessler's conclusion on the League's effect in the 1912 legislative election is that "there is no way of determining with accuracy that the anti-Asiatic issue was of basic importance in any of these campaigns."[56]

Failure of the League to gain a large political backing was due not only to party politics, but also to character, influence, and motivations of the League's major spokesman, Olaf Andrew Tveitmoe. The League was dissolved by 1913, due in part to his lack of leadership and his concern for other labor problems. An examination of the A. E. L., Proceedings, 1910-1913, shows that in 1910 he presided over seven of the monthly meetings and was absent during two meetings. In 1911, Tveitmoe called the meeting to order on five occasions, while the Vice President, E. B. Carr, presided over seven meetings. During 1912, Tveitmoe presided only at the March 17 meeting and did not appear again until March 16, 1913.[57]

---

[52]San Francisco Call, May 28, 1910, p. 5/4. What isn't mentioned at the League meetings is the fact that Walter Macarthur and Marc Anthony were opposing the above candidates for office, cf. San Francisco Call, May 28, 1910, p. 5/3; San Francisco Call, November 8, 1910, p. 8. Neither of them won in the election.

[53]Roger Daniels points out that while Bell openly courted the League, Johnson did everything but openly insult it. Daniels, op. cit., pp. 49-50. In the State primaries, Beban and Perrine were in competition for the senatorial seat of the twenty-fourth district. Three Republicans, Beban, Coglan, and Schmitt won their seats with large votes over their Democratic rivals, cf. Statement of the Vote, Election of November 8, 1910.

[54]Kessler, op. cit., pp. 64-65.

[55]Ibid., p. 66. Cf. also A. E. L., Proceedings, October 20, 1912, pp. 259-261, which contains a list of State legislators, dividing them into two groups: those who favor and those who do not favor legislation on the Japanese. Kessler states that not once during the entire year preceding the 1913 session of the legislature was there a single reference to the anti-Asiatic issues in the correspondence between Hiram Johnson and Mayor Lissner, the leader of Republican politics in Southern California, cf. Kessler, op. cit., p. 68, note 103.

[56]Ibid., p. 65.

[57]The single, bound volume of the A. E. L., Proceedings at the California Library in Sacramento is lacking the reports for July, August, and November 1910; January 1912. Not only was the March 1913 report the last in the volume, but each report tended to decrease in size by 1913.

Beginning in 1910, Tveitmoe not only became involved with other labor problems, but his involvement in the bombings of the Los Angeles Times on October 1, 1910, undoubtedly brought disrespect upon the League's goals. Not only was the Times anti-union, it was pro-Japanese. A Call editorial pointed out to San Franciscans that Harrison Gray Otis had published a half page article to demonstrate that Japanese in California were a "valuable asset for the state."[58] The day after the bombing Tveitmoe, as Secretary of the Building Trades Council, offered a $7,500 reward for the "apprehension of the guilty persons."[59] Within three weeks, Tveitmoe was involved in the bombing; and within a month, both he and Yoell were indicted by the Los Angeles grand jury.[60]

There was still one more explosion in Los Angeles. On Christmas night, 1910, a bomb wrecked part of the Llewellyn Iron Works, where union men were on strike.[61] It was this explosion which later implicated Tveitmoe in the conspiracy trials of 1912. A letter, addressed to J. J. McNamara, found by police and signed by Tveitmoe, stated: "Trusting that Santa Claus will be as kind and generous to you with surprises and presents of the season as he is to us in the Golden State, we beg to remain yours sincerely."[62]

San Francisco newspapers, especially the Call, hounded the labor leader with incessant questions and insinuations. One reporter asked Tveitmoe if he had written a letter to J. J. McNamara asking for the Indianapolis men to "send on your wreckers." Tveitmoe retorted:

> That is a lie, plain and simple. A lie, I tell you. No man who ever breathed ever saw that request written to any other man over my signature at any place, at any time. There never was such a

---

[58] San Francisco Call, January 16, 1910, p. 30/3.

[59] San Francisco Call, October 2, 1910, p. 2/2-4. When Tveitmoe was found guilty of conspiracy charges, detective Burns told newsmen that he was going to collect the reward from Tveitmoe, cf. San Francisco Call, January 3, 1912, p. 2/1. While Tveitmoe was involved in the Los Angeles bombings, he was absent from the annual State Building Trades Council meetings in January 1911 and 1913. In 1912, he spoke only of the Los Angeles trials. At none of the meetings following 1911 was there any mention of Japanese, cf. San Francisco Call, January 17, 1911, p. 4/5; San Francisco Call, January 16, 1912, p. 1/1; San Francisco Call, January 21, 1913, p. 8/1.

[60] San Francisco Call, October 22, 1910, p. 2/1; Sacramento Union, November 2, 1910, p. 1/4. Cf. also San Francisco Call, October 25, 1910, p. 2/3; San Francisco Chronicle, October 26, 1910, p. 1/7: Tveitmoe reported that he had met "Smitty and Caplan at the Asiatic Exclusion League headquarters." Both these men were suspected of being responsible for the dynamiting.

[61] Adamic, Dynamite, p. 213.

[62] San Francisco Call, February 16, 1912, p. 2/5; San Francisco Call, December 9, 1912, p. 3/2. Tveitmoe was also charged with acting as "paymaster" in handling the money for McNamara's defense and later with Clarence Darrow in handling the dynamiter's defense fund, San Francisco Call, October 9, 1912, p. 1/3.

letter and there is not now any such letter. That settles that.[63]

On another occasion, when Tveitmoe was returning from the Los Angeles trial of the McNamara brothers, he lost his temper with the Call reporter:

> 'You have pictured me as a thief, a robber, and a fugitive' he cried excitedly, his hands trembling and his face white. 'You have said that my wife had run away, that the telephone in our house had been disconnected, that I never would return to San Francisco. You have tried to make me out a murderer. You can now say anything and everything you wish, and my only answer is, and will be: You can all go to ....'[64]

In December 1912, Tveitmoe was found guilty of conspiracy for illegal transportation of explosives and aiding in the explosion of the Times.[65] For the second time in his life, Tveitmoe was dressed in gray prison uniforms. He began to serve his six-year sentence at Leavenworth, Kansas, January 2, 1913.[66]

William J. Burns, one of the most important prosecutors of the McNamaras, also defendants in the conspiracy trials, remarked that the conviction of Tveitmoe, "friend of Gompers and the brains behind the Los Angeles dynamiting was 'more important than all the others.'"[67] At Tveitmoe's trial, Burns told the Call reporter:

> I have reason to believe that it was Tveitmoe who suggested blowing up the Los Angeles Times building, that it was he who induced John J. McNamara to send his brother west to do the job. Tveitmoe is in a class by himself. He does not represent organized labor, but his own peculiar ideas and clan. It would be an insult to organized labor to speak of him as one of its representatives.[68]

While Tveitmoe's main concern was focused on the Los Angeles bombings, he brought further disrespect and suspicion on his character by involving union members, and undoubtedly League participants, in purchasing stock in the Sunset National Oil

---

[63] San Francisco Call, January 4, 1912, p. 1/7.

[64] San Francisco Call, December 17, 1911, p. 46/1; San Francisco Call, December 16, 1911, p. 10/1.

[65] San Francisco Call, December 29, 1912, p. 21/3; San Francisco Call, December 31, 1912, p. 2/7.

[66] San Francisco Call, January 3, 1913, p. 9/4. The San Francisco Building Trades Council passed a resolution the same day to "favor the sentiment now for the declaration of a general strike throughout the length and breadth of this nation," ibid., p. 9/5. Tveitmoe was released from prison March 2 on a $120,000 bond raised by union labor within thirteen days of his imprisonment, San Francisco Call, January 17, 1913, p. 5/4; San Francisco Call, March 3, 1913, p. 2/4.

[67] Adamic, op. cit., p. 247.

[68] San Francisco Call, December 29, 1912, p. 23/4.

Company.[69] The company was formed in June 1910, as the "million dollar union man's oil company."[70] Its management included O. A. Tveitmoe as President; Walter E. O'Connell, San Francisco Police Commissioner on the Advisory Board; J. B. Burns, Vice President of the State Building Trades Council; A. E. Yoell, of the Exclusion League, and a number of other prominent labor officials from San Francisco and Los Angeles.[71] The stock was advertised at twenty-five cents a share with the admonition that it would increase momentarily. The San Francisco Examiner reported that at least 400 workingmen subscribed and in only a few instances did each investor subscribe for less than 100 shares.[72] The company's prospectus stated:

> The Sunset National Oil Company is composed exclusively of men who have for many years successfully managed the affairs of the largest and strongest labor organizations. Men with records to be proud of. These men will protect the dollars you invest in the Sunset National Oil Company as carefully as they have guarded the labor interests for many years past .... Don't be backward about buying a small interest. If you cannot afford to invest over $25, buy that much anyway .... Remember, the men at the Company's head are not professional grafting brokers or promoters, but friends of yours.[73]

The Company was adjudged bankrupt on January 26,[74] shortly after former Mayor E. E. Schmitz and his Pan-American Oil Company were no longer able to "nurse the failing Sunset along."[75] Tveitmoe, as President of the company, appeared in the District Court and claimed that the liability amounted to $15,156 and the assets were $15,376.[76] Although he claimed to have loaned the company $2,714 to maintain solvency, fraud charges were later brought against him by the Associated Supply Company of San Francisco.[77]

---

[69] The legal formation of the company may be found in the California State Archives, Corporation #62171: Sunset National Oil Company, 29 June 1910, MS, Secretary of State, Inactive Corporation, RG, California State Archives, Sacramento.

[70] San Francisco Examiner, January 12, 1911, p. 1/7.

[71] Ibid., p. 2/1. Cress Gannon, the business manager of Organized Labor, was listed on the advisory board. Tveitmoe was editor of this journal. Cf. also San Francisco Examiner, January 13, 1911, p. 5/1.

[72] Ibid., p. 2/2.

[73] Ibid. These prospectus were widely circulated in June and July of 1910 and undoubtedly appeared in the major labor journals of San Francisco.

[74] San Francisco Examiner, January 26, 1911, p. 7/7.

[75] San Francisco Examiner, January 12, 1911, p. 1/7. One of the Sunset's advertisements mentioned that oil wells were being drilled by the "Schmitz Drilling Company," and that 2,500 barrels of oil were due by October 1, 1910. Ibid., p. 2/1.

[76] San Francisco Call, March 7, 1911, p. 19/5. Among the creditors listed is one for Organized Labor for $699, and one by the Labor Clarion for $200. The San Francisco Call on September 21, 1912, p. 12/5, reported that the Labor Clarion was run at a loss of $900 in 1911.

[77] San Francisco Examiner, September 14, 1911, p. 15/2.

While Tveitmoe was involved with court proceedings in the Times bombing as well as suits over the Sunset National Oil Company in 1911,[78] the Asiatic Exclusion League became involved in one of the most controversial political acts of its entire eight-year history. During January and February 1911, the Exclusion League sent several communications to the legislature and the Governor, asking that legislative bills dealing with the Japanese or other foreigners be delayed until the League and its allies had an opportunity to examine them.[79] On January 16, the State Building Trades Council adopted a unanimous resolution to A. H. Hewitt, Speaker of the Assembly:

> That this council immediately wire legislators at Sacramento requesting them to withhold any bills affecting Japanese or foreign citizens until representatives of State Council, State Federation of Labor, San Francisco, have an opportunity to analyze these measures in accordance with suggestions by Mayor McCarthy, which were communicated by the President of the Asiatic Exclusion League on December 26, 1910 [sic: December 16], to the members of the State legislature.[80]

A conference of labor lobbyists was held at labor legislative headquarters at Tenth and K Streets to assure the delay requested by the State Federation of Labor and affiliated bodies.[81] The State Building Trades Council met again on January 20 and received an address by Frank McGowan, who submitted recommendations from the League "that aliens be prohibited from holding land and be separated from white children in the public schools."[82]

These requests by the State Building Trades Council and the State Federation of Labor were ignored by Senator Thomas Finn, a Republican from San Francisco, who introduced Senate Bill 1074 on February 10, 1911, entitled "An Act to Regulate The Ownership or Possession of Lands By Aliens."[83] The Exclusion League quickly responded to the Assembly Speaker on February 13:

---

[78]To complicate matter even more, Tveitmoe broke his leg on February 5, 1911, and was hospitalized most of that month, cf. San Francisco Call, February 5, 1911, p. 37/5; San Francisco Call, February 24, 1911, p. 3/3.

[79]Letter, Tveitmoe to Johnson, January 16, 1911, Johnson Papers, cited in Kessler, op. cit., p. 31; cf. Assembly Journal, January 17, 1911, p. 191.

[80]Sacramento Union, January 18, 1911, p. 1/3. The meeting on December 16, 1910, was for the purpose of making arrangements "to bring the subject of Asiatic influx before the legislature," San Francisco Call, December 16, 1910, p. 14/2. Perhaps one of the reasons for this resolution was that P. H. McCarthy was in Washington attempting to bring the Panama-Pacific Exposition to San Francisco, cf. San Francisco Call, January 19, 1911, p. 1/3.

[81]Ibid.

[82]San Francisco Call, January 20, 1911, p. 3/1. No action seems to have been taken on his recommendation, San Francisco Call, January 21, 1911, p. 11/4.

[83]Tom Finn later became sheriff of San Francisco and was a local party boss for Hiram Johnson. S. C. Olin, op. cit., p. 133. The Finn Bill is in Appendix A of this paper. Cf. Senate Journal, February 10, 1911, p. 781. The Finn Bill, 1074, along with Senate bills 2, 24, and 167, were all sent to the Assembly and were never reported out of committee, Senate Journal, p. 2364.

> The executive board of the Asiatic Exclusion League regrets that
> regardless of previous communication on the subject we have not
> been afforded an opportunity to examine the Anti-Alien Asiatic
> bills which you introduced in the Senate Friday. It is the sense
> of the board that such bills as these at the present time are
> not conducive to the final enactment of effective and permanent
> Asiatic exclusion legislation and which only can be had through
> Act of Congress. The school segregation question has for some
> years been fairly satisfactorily settled and alien land tenure
> is judiciously and sanely dealt with by this league and the State
> labor bodies. We respectfully request that you proceed cautiously
> in this matter, as pressing measures of this kind now would mean
> irreparable injury to the exclusion cause.[84]

The letter was signed by O. A. Tveitmoe and A. E. Yoell, but it was probably written by Yoell who met with the League delegates on February 19. A controversy developed among the delegates, especially Finn's friends, who wanted to know the reasons why the executive committee sent the telegram in the first place. Yoell, spokesman for the executive committee, declared that Finn had ulterior motives in presenting the bill while Finn's friends maintained that the telegram was a piece of politics to injure the Senator. Yoell's explanation for sending the telegram was that

> Finn doesn't know anything about exclusion ... he doesn't even
> know the text of his own bills, I'll bet you. I don't criticize
> the bills, but I criticize Finn's motives in presenting them. It
> is just a scheme for cheap notoriety to further his own ends.[85]

At one point, according to the Call reporter, the orator became so impassioned that the head of the Chairman's gavel flew off and shot across the room. One delegate, John Keane, told Yoell, "that telegram you sent has been a detriment to the whole movement."[86] A vote was taken to eliminate the telegram from the report of the League's Proceedings, thereby vindicating Finn.[87]

---

[84] Assembly Journal (Extra Session, 1910), 1911, p. 700. Cf. also Kessler, op. cit., p. 32; Yamato Ichihaski, Japanese in the United States, pp. 263-264; Hichborn, Legislation of 1911, p. 344; Daniels, op. cit., p. 52. Daniels refers to the letter as a voltiface which ended the League's effective influence on the legislature, an idea which he must have absorbed from Hichborn: "... the influence of labor in Anti-Alien legislation had clearly been weakened by the action of San Francisco labor leaders two years before in requesting the defeat in the Assembly of the Anti-Asiatic Land Bill after it had passed the Senate, Hichborn, Legislature of 1913, p. 225.

[85] San Francisco Call, February 20, 1911, p. 4/5.

[86] Ibid. Keane was the chief deputy in the office of the State Commissioner of Labor, San Francisco Call, April 13, 1913, p. 49/4. J. B. Kessler believed that the telegram "diminished the effectiveness of Labor's appeal for the enactment of an anti-Alien land law in 1913." Kessler, op. cit., p. 70. One of the League delegates, George B. Benham, later commented, "I do not personally subscribe to the action of this organization in withdrawing from the fight at Sacramento for the exclusion bill. The time is now, and we must heed it. Otherwise war will follow," San Francisco Call, April 17, 1911, p. 14/1.

[87] Ibid. The vote was nineteen in favor of dropping the telegram from the report to twelve against. The Proceedings for February 1911, contains a statement of the

Within a week of the League's meeting, Assemblyman Harry Polsey wrote Tveitmoe asking why the organization had reversed its position on Japanese legislation. Tveitmoe's response tends to further confuse the intent of the telegram.

> The circular letters sent you represent 70,000 members of the State Building Trades Council of San Francisco and I therefore appreciate the fact that you will give the matter 'due consideration.' I am not seeking consideration of you or any other member of the legislature, office holder, or politician from a personal standpoint, and your worry over what you term my breakdown on Japanese legislation is therefore not only erroneous, but entirely misplaced. The circulars were sent because there were two bills pending in the legislature affecting Japanese legislation[88] which had been endorsed by labor organizations, and the more drastic bills of Senator Finn would only retard their passage.[89]

It is little wonder that Franklin Hichborn, Assemblyman Polsey, and Governor Johnson became confused on the League's purpose, for only two months after the Finn "circular letter" the Exclusion League countered its actions by denouncing the legislature for failing to pass an anti-alien land bill. Yoell began the League meeting by bitterly attacking the action of the Judiciary Committee for allowing the alien land bill to die in its files.

> It is the worst of unfair treatment this state has seen for many sessions. The bill was killed during a secret meeting after it had been reported favorably. The action of some of the reform legislators was cowardly. Although they refused to either vote or speak against it, they took refuge in reprehensible political methods.[90]

It seems fairly certain that in the first few months of 1911, the League lacked the guiding presence of Tveitmoe's leadership. While both he and Yoell attempted to justify the Finn "circular letter" on the basis of party politics, there is evidence for another more important motive.

Executive Board which concludes: "Our fight for exclusion will be won at Washington. That fight for the Alien land tenure bill is going to be carried on at Sacramento until it is won," A. E. L., Proceedings, February 20, 1911, p. 87.

[88]There were three bills introduced to the Senate and sent to the Assembly dealing with alien land rights--besides the Finn bill: SB 2, Larkin; SB 24, Sanford; SB 167, Larkin, cf. Senate Journal, Extra Session, 1910, pp. 95, 98, 124.

[89]San Francisco Call, February 26, 1911, p. 33/1. Tveitmoe had previously stated that the Finn and Sanford bills were similar. "It is difficult to understand why he would censure one by implication and not the other. Careful examination of the evidence make Tveitmoe's defense of his actions appear to be a non sequitur," Kessler, op. cit., p. 33, note 31.

[90]San Francisco Call, April 16, 1911, p. 91/2. Cf. Hichborn, Legislature of 1911, p. 342. It is worth noting that Tveitmoe was absent from the February 20 League meeting, and on April 16, he left San Francisco for the labor trials of Los Angeles.

P. H. McCarthy, Mayor of San Francisco, was in Washington during January and February 1911, on a "mission of the greatest moment to labor, since its object was to bring the Panama-Pacific exposition to San Francisco."[91] It was the goal of the Panama-Pacific Company to take an active part in stopping the Alien land bills in the 1911 legislature. A telegram was circulated among the members of the Assembly which stated:

> On behalf of the Panama-Pacific International Exposition Company we [James McNab, Chairman of California's Legislative Committee] emphatically protest against the passage of the Alien Land Law Senate bill as it is at present drawn, believing that the passage of this bill would work great injury to the exposition and we respectfully ask your best efforts to defeat it.[92]

The final contract between the San Francisco Building Trades Council and the Panama-Pacific Exposition was drawn up on August 12, 1912. P. H. McCarthy, O. A. Tveitmoe, J. P. McLaughlin, and J. I. Nolan signed as representatives of the Building Trades and the Labor Council of San Francisco.[93] Article seven stated that if workmen were brought by any of the foreign exhibitors, the Building Trades and the Labor Council would "co-operate with said workmen in performing all work required and in no case will there be any discrimination against the said workmen."[94]

James D. Phelan undoubtedly assisted McCarthy's efforts in Washington for like McCarthy, Phelan was willing to "modify" his anti-Japanese agitation long enough to secure the exposition site for San Francisco.[95] He gloated over the fact that

---

[91] San Francisco Call, January 19, 1911, p. 1/3; The Panama-Pacific Exposition was McCarthy's major concern in 1911, as well as his claim to fame, San Francisco Call, March 24, 1911, p. 14/1. Daniels claims that McCarthy used his influence to halt the anti-Japanese agitation, at least temporarily, in exchange for the support of the national administration's backing of San Francisco as the location for the exposition, Daniels, op. cit., p. 51, note 28, citing Taft and Knox MSS.

[92] F. Hichborn, Legislature of 1911, p. 342. During the hearings on Japanese Immigration in 1920, Dr. H. B. Johnson, one of the most outspoken defenders of Japanese rights in California, recommended Hichborn's account of the exposition efforts. "In the earlier years the trouble grew out of the agitation on the part of the labor unions, but when the head of the exposition found that it would be absolutely necessary to have some kind of an agreement with the labor organizations or it would be absolutely impossible for a successful putting through of the exposition, and during that time there was a cessation of activities on the part of the labor organizations." Hearings on Japanese Immigration, 1920, p. 584.

[93] The contract is in the files of the State Building Trades Council of California, San Francisco. Cited in F. L. Ryan, op. cit., p. 208.

[94] Ibid., p. 216. Articles eight, fifteen, and sixteen also apply to the reasons for the exposition's protest of the alien legislation in 1913.

[95] Even while the League was engaged in the controversy over the Finn "circular letter," Phelan spoke on the Japanese immigration issue while dedicating the foundation stone of the Native Son's hall, San Francisco Call, February 23, 1911, p. 2/2. On April 2, 1913, Phelan appeared before the Joint Senate and Assembly Judiciary Committee and stated: "The future of California is of far greater importance than the success of this exposition. And in saying this, I

The Japanese government has a site adjoining the Presidio where it is going to put $1,000,000 in a building an in beautifying the grounds after the Japanese fashion and this property, after the exposition, will revert to the federal government and add much to the beauty of the federal reserve there.[96]

Once San Francisco was assured of the exposition site, the League again began circulating its publications for anti-Japanese legislation at both state and federal levels. In the June 1911 meeting, a special committee appointed by the Exclusion League presented a bill to regulate immigration of aliens into the United States. The committee, consisting of Frank McGowan, Theodore A. Bell, William A. Cole, O. A. Tveitmoe, and A. E. Yoell, prepared a bill after careful examination of all the general immigration laws. The bill was designed to deal with all Asiatics instead of classifying racial origins.[97] This bill was presented in the House of Representatives by California's Democratic Representative, John E. Raker, who was a "proponent of the most stringent type of exclusion legislation and a friend of the Asiatic Exclusion League."[98] As a Congressman from the First District, Raker presented H. R. 13,500 first in 1911 while the League made every effort to secure Congressional approval throughout 1912.[99] Although Raker was not able to pass his

---

do not believe for a moment that in enacting this land legislation you will jeopardize the success of the exposition," Hichborn, Legislature of 1913, p. 234.

[96]San Francisco Call, December 8, 1912, p. 26/1. Phelan, a diplomatic master of double talk, even attempted to gloss over the race riots in San Francisco's Japanese restaurants as "not of race prejudice, but simply the objection of union labor people to white men patronizing a restaurant run on a non-union basis by those supposed to be hostile to union labor .... As for any outbreak against the Japanese having occurred, there was none at all. There will be no race war in San Francisco and the Japanese there will receive abundant protection." San Francisco Call, June 12, 1907, p. 10/2. Cf. Bailey, Roosevelt and the Japanese-American Crisis for a more objective view of the riot.

[97]San Francisco Call, June 19, 1911, p. 17/6. The League had also received communications from State Senators Perkins and Works on recommendations for appointment of a new immigration inspector. The Senators proposed Samuel W. Backus while Yoell claimed Backus was not qualified on the basis of experience. Yoell thought Luther C. Stewart, present acting inspector, was best qualified for the job.

[98]Kessler, op. cit., p. 128. The draft of the committee's statement is in A. E. L., Proceedings, June 18, 1911, p. 121. The Baker Bill, HR 13,500, is in United States Congressional Record, 62nd Congress, First Session, 1911, XLVII, Part 4, p. 3858. Other Congressmen who had pledged themselves to support exclusion legislation were: William Kent, Sylvester C. Smith, Julius Kahn, James C. Needham, E. A. Hayes, and Joseph R. Knowland, J. B. Kessler, op. cit., p. 48.

[99]Baker, before the election of 1910, was a Superior Court Judge in Alturas. Sacramento Bee, September 27, 1910, p. 16/2. Cf. Hearings on Japanese Immigration, 1920, p. 498.

immigration bill in 1912, he promised the League "that every effort is being made to put through House bill 13,500 at the next session of Congress."[100]

With frustrations mounting in Congress over the defeat of the Raker Bill, the League again intensified its efforts on the State legislature to obtain an Alien land law. Like the Raker Bill, the League wrote its own bill to be presented to the legislature.[101] Perhaps more than any other factor, it was this bill, and its contents, especially section eight, which was to cause disintegration of the League in 1913. The section stated that "every contract agreement or lease of any land made with or to any Alien not eligible to citizenship under the laws of the United States shall be null and void."[102]

After the December 1912, meeting, the League began to gather information to prove its claim that the "Japs own and control fertile valley land equal to a strip five miles in width and as long as the State of California."[103] At the January meeting, the executive board reported on returns from nineteen out of the fifty-eight counties in California showing Japanese and Chinese property holdings. Asiatic land holdings, claimed the League, amounted to better than 6,997 acres owned by 498 Asiatics with an assessed valuation of $1,105,611.[104] The League was

---

[100]San Francisco Call, January 20, 1913, p. 14/5. Tveitmoe solicited support of Samuel Gompers in behalf of the Raker Bill. A. E. L., Proceedings, May 19, 1912, p. 225. At the following meeting, Yoell complained of opposition from the Chinese Six Companies, San Francisco Chamber of Commerce, and John P. Irish, Secretary of the Delta Association--an organization of agricultural producers at the confluence of the Sacramento and San Joaquin Rivers, A. E. L., Proceedings, June 16, 1912, p. 229. Irish, like H. B. Johnson, was an outspoken defender of Japanese rights in California and was V. S. McClatchy's main opposition in 1919-1920. In a letter to Charles W. Eliot, former President of Harvard University, Irish proudly claimed that he had played a major part in securing the defeat of an immigration bill session of Congress before 1912, Irish Papers, May 27, 1912, Stanford University, cited in Kessler, op. cit., p. 43.

[101]A. E. L., Proceedings, December 15, 1912, pp. 278-279. The bill was sent to the legislature along with the Proceedings for January and February 1913, A. E. L., Proceedings, March 16, 1913, p. 299.

[102]Ibid., p. 279. The complete League bill is in Appendix B of this paper.

[103]Ibid.

[104]San Francisco Call, January 20, 1913, p. 14/5. The San Francisco Call later published figures on Japanese property ownership based on tables of the 15th Biennial Report of State Labor Statistics, p. 633, which stated the total amount of land owned by Japanese in 1912 was 12,726 acres or twenty square miles ... the Japanese owned but 1/2,000 of [the state]. There are some 58,000 Japanese forming 2.32% of the population of the state. These facts clearly show that the Japanese neither own much land nor have they a visible tendency to purchase land," San Francisco Call, May 3, 1913, p. 3/5. Hamilton Holt, editor of the Independent claimed that 30,000 Japanese owned 17,000 acres of land, San Francisco Call, May 7, 1913, p. 5/7. In an open letter to Congressman Raker, J. B. Sanford claimed "Japs own 52,000 acres of land, lease 400,000 acres." San Francisco Call, April 10, 1913, cited in Kessler, op. cit., p. 128.

convinced that enough information had been gathered "to prove to the legislators that it is necessary to enact a law forbidding Asiatics from acquiring more lands in the state."[105] The executive board urged affiliated organizations to lend their voice and votes in favor of Senate Bill 27 introduced by Senator J. B. Sanford. The League insisted on the Sanford Bill even if its passage meant war.[106]

During February, March, and April, the League refused to modify its position on land leases by Asiatics. Indeed, when the legislature began to favor bills with lease options, the League retaliated by making plans to invoke the initiative. Through representatives in Sacramento, the League wanted a resolution introduced "placing decisions of the matter in the hands of the voters of California ... [since] nothing has been done toward the enactment of a measure which will effectively prevent Japanese from purchasing land in California."[107]

The League was not alone in its efforts to block Orientals from leasing land. In January, it had sent communications to San Francisco labor councils asking for endorsement of the League's position.[108] At the San Francisco Labor Council meeting on May 2, 1913, delegates Paul Scharrenberg and C. H. McConaughey offered a resolution which would forever bar the "Asiatic hordes" from permanent settlement upon California soil. The Council asked legislators:

> Regardless of party affiliations, to support and further strengthen this bill [The Webb-Henry Bill] by providing that after three years from the date the law goes into effect [August 10, 1913] the privilege of leasing agricultural lands, which is in a modified form granted to said Aliens ineligible to citizenship, shall terminate.[109]

Shortly after the passage of the Alien Land Law by the legislature, Theodore Bell joined the League's effort to instigate the Initiative and Referendum to obtain

---

[105]San Francisco Call, January 20, 1913, p. 14/5.

[106]A. E. L., Proceedings, February 17, 1913, pp. 293-294. If Sanford had taken Marc Anthony's place in the Senate as the League's representative, the Senator was not looked upon very favorably by Governor Johnson who saw him as "a blustering demagogue, his chief stock in trade--the Japanese question," Letter of H. W. Johnson to T. Roosevelt, June 21, 1913, cited in Daniels, op. cit., p. 116. Such a description was to fit the character of Jack M. Inman, Senator from Sacramento in the 1919-1920 legislature.

[107]San Francisco Call, April 21, 1913, p. 16/2. On May 3, Senator Boynton added a three-year lease privilege to the Henry Webb Bill so that Japanese laborers would remain in the state and not bring a shortage in the labor supply, San Francisco Call, May 3, 1913, p. 1/1; cf. Hichborn, Legislature of 1913, pp. 268-269.

[108]San Francisco Call, January 25, 1913, p. 5/5.

[109]San Francisco Call, May 3, 1913, p. 10/4. In attendance at this council meeting were Andrew J. Gallagher, President of the Council, P. H. McCarthy, and John P. McLaughlin--all of whom were League members.

an expression from the voters since "the three-year leasing clause makes the bill unsatisfactory to California and Japan alike."[110] Bell proposed three measures which surely would have confused most voters, but were geared to satisfy all factions.

> Through the Initiative we shall propose two laws for The People to vote on at the general election in November 1914, or at a special election which the Governor is authorized to call--one a general Alien land law applicable to all Aliens, and the other a measure similar to Senate Bill Five (the measure before the Governor) without the leasing clause. In addition thereto, Senate Bill Five should go to a Referendum vote at the same election. This would give The People three measures to choose from, and then the electors of California can once and for all enact an alien bill that will meet the demands of a majority of our people.[111]

The following day, Governor Johnson charged the Democrats with indulging in mere pretense and hypocrisy. He stated that "these gentlemen who are now speaking of referendum sought by every means in their power to prevent any law at all. By filibustering and by a resolution for delay they endeavored to prevent action."[112] Bell and the Democrats maintained their position that if Johnson signed the bill, "referendum petitions will be in circulation all over the state within a few hours. They are already printed and ready for distribution and it will be only a matter of a short time before the necessary 20,000 signatures are obtained."[113]

Hiram Johnson was not impressed with threats from the Democrats or a referendum movement and signed the Alien Land Law on May 19, 1913. The day before Johnson signed the bill, the League met at Labor Temple, San Francisco, and attacked the bill as "a gold brick thinly veiled with tin and compiled by partisan politicians to defeat the ultimate cause of exclusion."[114] The Executive Committee began to prepare a referendum and initiative for circulation.[115] Johnson countered the League's threat with a statement on the day following his signing of the bill into law:

> California for the first time in its history has an alien land law. Any man who wishes another kind of law may consistently invoke the initiative. No man who really wishes an alien land law will sign a referendum as to this law.[116]

---

[110]Sacramento Bee, May 7, 1913, p. 4/1. Just three days before, W. J. Bryan, Secretary of State, had left Sacramento in defeat of his and Wilson's attempt to make the law applicable to all Aliens. One of Bryan's last comments was that he looked "to the people of the state to express a final judgment, through the referendum, before the Act shall go into effect," Sacramento Union, May 4, 1913, p. 1/1.

[111]Sacramento Bee, May 7, 1913, p. 4/1.

[112]San Francisco Call, May 8, 1913, p. 3/6; cf. also San Francisco Call, May 9, 1913, p. 1/2.

[113]San Francisco Call, May 12, 1913, p. 1/6.

[114]San Francisco Call, May 19, 1913, p. 2/2.

[115]San Francisco Call, May 20, 1913, p. 2/1.

[116]San Francisco Call, May 20, 1913, p. 1/7.

The Governor became even more insistent against those who would invoke the referendum as "recreant to his citizenship and violates every tenet between man and man."[117]

The effect of these verbal missiles from Johnson were to prove to be the coup de grace' for the Asiatic Exclusion League. Even before the passage of the Webb Bill, other protest groups arose to challenge the League. The Anti-Alien Land Owner's League of Northern San Joaquin County was formed in the last week of April 1913. The Bee reported that the Lodi League had taken a leading part in the anti-alien legislation and had commenced the circulation of a petition to recall the five million dollars voted by the state for the support of the 1915 Exposition because of San Francisco's "attitude on the management of the anti-alien question."[118] The Exclusion League began to lose backing by certain labor unions in May 1913. Unions in Los Angeles, Stockton, Pasadena, Oakland, Alameda, Berkeley, and Santa Clara sent communications to the Senate urging passage of the Webb Bill.[119]

The split in the League's ranks continued throughout May 1913, when the Secretary of the San Jose Branch of the Building Trades Council, Walter G. Mathewson, wrote to Johnson in apparent approval of the Webb Act. In an open letter to Walter Mathewson, Johnson could only hope to further drive a wedge into the League's opposition.

> I was glad to get your note of May 23 with a copy of the resolutions of your Building Trades Council. I have been shocked and horrified at the attitude of some of the labor people of San Francisco, but I am proud to say that those labor leaders whom we respect have taken the same position that your people in Santa Clara County have taken.
>
> We have done the big thing in this alien land legislation. We have laid the ghost that has been with us so many years and we have gone ahead and legislated on a subject that it was our legal and moral right to legislate upon. We have started in the right direction and we have a good law, which, it may be asserted, does not go far enough, but which, at any rate, goes forward in the line that we desire; and any man who claims to favor an alien land law that will sign a referendum against this law is either an idiot, or is bought .... This particular law that we have passed and that I have signed is one of the most drastic laws upon the subject that ever has been introduced by the California legislature. Every other bill that has been before the legislature in the past 8 years provided in one fashion or another for leasing, and the only two bills that were seriously discussed during Mr. Bryan's stay here provided not only for leasing of land, but for the right to purchase, and hold for a limited period as well.[120]

---

[117]San Francisco Call, May 28, 1913, p. 18/1.

[118]Sacramento Bee, April 29, 1913, p. 5/1.

[119]Senate Journal, May 1, 1913, p. 2224; May 2, p. 2304.

[120]San Francisco Call, May 27, 1913, p. 4/2.

It was not only the Governor, the Progressive Republicans, and certain factions in the Building Trades Council that denounced the Exclusion League for its position on the Alien land law, but members of the League's executive board as well. It seems that H. F. McMahon, President of the Anti-Japanese Laundry League, had formed another organization entitled the Associated Anti-Japanese League. It was this League which joined the growing opposition to the Exclusion League on the basis "that by invoking the referendum the Exclusion League would threaten the nullification, for two years at least, of the new law and encourage and assist the Oriental to acquire California land."[121] McMahon paraphrased the Governor's statement that the "alien land law, while not all that is hoped for ultimately, is the successful culmination of an eight years' struggle and a tremendous stride in the work of retaining upon this soil the white man's standard."[122] Other unions joined in with the dissent.[123]

It seems fairly certain that the Governor was successful in stopping the referendum movement, but the Exclusion League survived for several months after the Governor signed the bill into law.[124] However, before the Webb Act went into effect on August 10, 1913, the League reversed its position on the alien land law, perhaps for the last time.

> Such laws as those passed by California are good and wise laws, and every state ought to adopt the same policy, for it is one of the worst calamities that can befall a country to have any considerable portion of its land or other natural resources owned and controlled by foreigners, whether resident or nonresident—and this being true, irrespective of differences of races. But when such foreign ownership also involves a race question, the evil is aggravated tenfold.[125]

The League seemed to gain little attention or backing from the unions after May 1913. The League had, however, served its purpose in keeping bills before Congress which were never passed in its eight years of existence. The League was only successful, ironically, in gaining recognition from the California legislature which passed a land law disliked, in part, by the League. It was the League, and its leaders, who engaged in party-politics, and it was the legislature and its "progressive" leaders who passed a discriminating law against those ineligible to citizenship that was to remain on the books for nearly forty years. The responsibility for the passage of the Alien Land Law of 1913 ultimately rests on the politicians, especially those who played at party politics and those who sought social recognition and political promotions.

---

[121] San Francisco Call, May 30, 1913, p. 4/1.

[122] Ibid. McMahon characterized the Exclusion League as "a form minus a remnant of prestige."

[123] In Sacramento, the Federated Trades Council adopted a strong resolution in opposition to the proposed referendum, San Francisco Call, June 1, 1913, p. 27/5.

[124] The Exclusion League met again on July 12, and August 18, 1913.

[125] San Francisco Call, July 12, 1913, p. 12/2. The Executive Board also recommended that the leasing of land by aliens not eligible to citizenship be submitted to the voters of the state for approval.

CHAPTER IV

THE ORIGINS OF THE ALIEN LAND LAW: FACTS AND MYTHS

Not by antipathy, but by sympathy; not by hostility, but by hospitality; not by enmity, but by amity, does one race come to know the heart of another.

    "Doctor Jordan Chides America," <u>San Francisco Call</u>, May 25, 1913, p. 27/5.

CHAPTER IV

THE ORIGINS OF THE ALIEN LAND LAW: FACTS AND MYTHS

Passage of the Alien Land Law, or Webb-Henry Bill, by the California Legislature on May 3, 1913, was the result of party politics and misunderstandings between a Progressive Democratic Federal Government and a Progressive Republican State administration. Caught between these political giants was a small, non-voting minority--"ineligible to citizenship"--who found themselves being discriminated against on the basis of racial origin.[1] Despite the propaganda and myths spread by the Exclusion League, labor unions, politicians, and certain newspapers, the Japanese minority was small when compared to the citizen population. There will always be a dispute over the Japanese population in the United States. The Exclusion League's figures were taken from government sources based on fiscal returns which were converted into monthly and annual totals, but seldom included Japanese emigration during the period. The Department of Labor, under Secretary Straus, wrote to the League defending his figures for November 1, 1907, to October 31, 1908. In that period, claimed Straus, immigration amounted to 6,017, while the departures were 5,832, "leaving an increase for immigration of Japanese for that year of 185."[2]

The Department of Commerce and Labor printed immigration figures in its annual reports. The report in 1915 lists the immigration for each fiscal year to 1915 by races. The figures for Japanese immigration in Table 25 were:

1899	3,395	1905	11,021	1911	4,575
1900	12,628	1906	14,243	1912	6,172
1901	5,249	1907	30,824	1913	8,302
1902	14,455	1908	16,418	1914	8,941
1903	20,041	1909	3,275	1915	8,609[3]
1904	14,382	1910	2,798		

In 1919, at the height of the organized movement against the Japanese, the Commissioner General of Immigration pointed out that immigration statistics on the Japanese began in 1861. Breaking the figures down into decades, the Commissioner General illustrated the following increase of Japanese immigrants in the United States:

1860-1869	137	1890-1899	13,998
1870-1879	193	1900-1909	139,712
1880-1889	1,583	1910-1919	77,125[4]

---

[1]The land law applied primarily to immigrant Japanese, but it also applied to those Chinese in the state who had not been born in the United States, cf. Senate Journal, April 22, 1913, p. 1772.
[2]San Francisco Call, January 29, 1909, p. 2/7; cf. also San Francisco Call, September 9, 1907, p. 2/4; San Francisco Call, February 12, 1909, p. 4/5.
[3]Bureau of Immigration, Annual Report of the Commissioner General of Immigration to the Secretary of Labor, 1915, pp. 122, 156.
[4]Bureau of Immigration, Annual Report of the Commissioner General of Immigration to the Secretary of Labor, 1919, p. 55.

The Commissioner also included the statistics for the increased numbers of Japanese listed in the census records.

1870	73	1900	24,788
1880	401	1910	67,744[5]
1890	2,292		

He noted that immigration figures included the movement to Hawaii, as well as to the mainland since 1900, while the census figures related only to the continental United States.

Until 1913, the Asiatic Exclusion League and certain newspapers seem to have been the strongest critics of the government's figures. The League claimed that Japanese were smuggled into the country on ships; over the Mexican and Canadian borders; or were migrating from Hawaii.[6] Shortly after the San Francisco school incident, the League collected statistics on Japanese population in California. It found that the Japanese population in twenty-eight counties amounted to 15,000 in 1906, and had increased to more than 23,000 by October 1907. The total number of Japanese in the state was estimated at about 70,000, and of these only 123 individuals were on the assessment rolls, "showing clearly the status of [property ownership by] the Oriental in the state."[7] A survey of four bay cities by the California Promotion Committee revealed that there were about 4,500 Chinese and 5,500 Japanese in the area. The Call declared "the figures on the Orientals are admittedly most conservative."[8]

During the Alien Land Law controversy of 1913, the Call published an article on "Oriental Census Figures: Japanese in California." The Japanese population in San Francisco was reported to be 6,900; in Alameda County, 4,400; in Contra Costa,

---

[5]Ibid. The Japanese population in the California census was 10,151 in 1900; 41,356 in 1910, and 71,952 in 1920. United States Census Report, 1920, III, Table 7, "Changes in Numbers of Chinese and Japanese Population in California 1900, 1910, 1920," pp. 109-110, quoted in Walter Beach, Oriental Crime in California, pp. 14-15. Governor W. D. Stephens maintained that the Japanese population was 87,279 in 1920 and this figure constituted eighty to eighty-five percent of the total Japanese population in the United States, California and the Oriental, p. 8.

[6]San Francisco Call, June 15, 1907, p. 4/6; San Francisco Call, September 9, 1907, p. 2/4; San Francisco Call, December 16, 1907, p. 2/3; San Francisco Call, July 21, 1910, p. 4/3.

[7]San Francisco Call, October 14, 1907, p. 7/2. The League published a population count of Japanese and Chinese in seventeen counties in the San Francisco Call, September 9, 1907, p. 2/4. The League later received information that the 800 Japanese reported by Sonoma County officials was an attempt to mislead the League. A canvass of seventy-eight farms was made and it was found that "nearly twice as many Orientals were employed in the county," San Francisco Call, October 14, 1907, p. 7/2.

[8]San Francisco Call, November 7, 1907, p. 10/1. The League claimed the Japanese population in San Francisco was 13,685, San Francisco Call, September 9, 1907, p. 2/4.

1,000; in San Mateo, 350; with a total of 12,650 for the bay district. The Japanese population in the state was estimated at 58,000, of which 47,500 were men, 6,400 women, and 4,100 children.[9]

In contrast to the racist oriented Exclusion League was the Japanese Society of America. Its members adopted a resolution

> to placate the ire of the labor interests of the coast which have been aroused against the importation of coolie labor .... We have prepared this petition looking to the [exclusion] of this class in order to anticipate and prevent the radical exclusion of the Japanese as a race from this country.[10]

It was this social organization which was to form part of the main opposition protesting as prejudicial in nature the actions and publications of the Asiatic Exclusion League.

Formed just a little over five months after the Exclusion League, its stated purpose was to study the arts of Old Japan and arouse an interest in its people, the Nipponese, while attempting to promote a cordial relationship with the people of that country. Its first officers were Henry P. Bowie, President; David Starr Jordan, Vice President; and Ralph C. Harrison, Second Vice President.[11] About fifty people signed the enrollment card, including a number of prominent individuals from the local Japanese colony, reported the Call. Later, a formal constitution was drawn up to state the purpose of the society whose membership had grown to exceed two hundred.[12] By midyear, 1907, the society had established a branch in New York City where some of the most prominent citizens joined the society. Its President was John H. Finley, President of New York City College; Honorary President was Viscount Aoki, and its membership included Admiral Thomas Dewey, Fred D. Grant, August Belmont, Hamilton Holt, and others.[13]

---

[9]San Francisco Call, April 22, 1913, p. 2/2. The most comprehensive study on Japanese statistics in California of 1912 may be found in Appendix of the Journals of the Senate and Assembly of the 40th Session of the Legislature of the State of California, Report of the Bureau of Labor Statistics, "Japanese Statistics," III, 1913, pp. 604-637.

[10]San Francisco Call, February 3, 1907, p. 23/2.

[11]San Francisco Call, October 8, 1905, p. 37/3. One of the corresponding secretaries was Taku Matsu Mikee Moto. The second president of the association was K. Kadico, San Francisco Call, October 26, 1906, p. 5/2. Theodore Roosevelt accepted the invitation of D. S. Jordan to become the society's first honorary member, San Francisco Call, January 9, 1906, p. 9/2.

[12]San Francisco Call, January 9, 1906, p. 9/2; San Francisco Call, January 22, 1906, p. 9/5.

[13]San Francisco Call, May 20, 1907, p. 2/6. D. S. Jordan, under constant attack both by the League and the San Francisco Call (cf. San Francisco Call, January 22, 1907, p. 1/3 headline: "Anti-Japanese Order Issued by Jordan") was the most outspoken defender of Japanese rights in California along with John P. Irish. Even during the alien land law controversy, Jordan sent a letter to President Wilson commending the latter's efforts to stop discriminating legislation. Others who backed Jordan and the Japanese Society were Andrew Carnegie, Jacob H. Schiff, Charles W. Eliot, former Mayor Seth Low, and Lloyd C. Griscom, former ambassador to Italy; all were executive members of the society, San Francisco Call, April 26, 1913, p. 1/3.

A second, and more politically powerful organization, called the Japanese Association of America, was formed first in 1904 and incorporated under California's law on August 4, 1907.[14] Until the Japanese Agricultural Association of California was organized in 1915, the Japanese Association formed one of the major oppositions to the Exclusion League. Its purpose was to promote Japanese welfare in America. To this end, it sent letters of protest and passed resolutions which presumed to represent the opinions of large numbers of (but not necessarily all) Japanese in the United States.[15] The Association's President was K. Abiko; its Secretary was Gorouka Ikeda, a Columbia graduate; its Treasurer was K. Uyeda. The Association's regional headquarters was located at 444 Bush, San Francisco. By February 1907, the Association had twenty-three chapters in the state to assist Japanese farmers and businessmen.[16]

One President of the Japanese Association was George Shima, known by his contemporaries as the "Potato King." Perhaps more than any other Japanese agriculturalist--businessman, Shima overcame racial discrimination. Having faced and survived many crop failures and floods in the delta before 1905, Shima successfully reclaimed a large tract of land in the San Joaquin Delta region, just west of Stockton. Experimenting in potato planting, as well as attending the University of California at Berkeley,[17] Shima built and expanded his business on 4,000 acres of delta land which yielded 500,000 sacks of tubers at $200,000 profit by 1910.[18] His

---

[14] San Francisco Call, February 2, 1907, p. 2/3; Hearings on Japanese Immigration, 1920, p. 642. The Association claimed to be self-perpetuating body with no political or financial relationship with the Japanese government.

[15] The Association, along with the Japanese Imperial Council, K. Uyem, protested the actions of the San Francisco Board of Education in segregating Japanese students from the public schools as "discrimination that is unfair," San Francisco Call, October 19, 1906, p. 10/3; San Francisco Call, July 3, 1907, p. 2/4.

[16] San Francisco Call, February 2, 1907, p. 2/3. The Association's representatives from Sacramento and San Francisco were S. Takesaki and M. Tsukamoto, San Francisco Call, June 15, 1907, p. 4/6; San Francisco Call, September 23, 1908, p. 8/1. The association had well over fifty chapters by the end of the First World War, San Francisco Examiner, November 23, 1918, p. 11/5.

[17] When Shima purchased property at the corner of Parker and College Avenue in Berkeley, some of the residents protested vigorously. He built a home there in 1909, engaged tutors to educate his children, and contributed money to the university for a student infirmary which would be open for Japanese and American students who needed medical attention, San Francisco Call, March 13, 1909, p. 12/6; San Francisco Call, March 31, 1909, p. 8/4.

[18] San Francisco Call, December 16, 1910, p. 18/2; San Francisco Chronicle, January 6, 1914, p. 13/3. Cf. Shima's testimony in Hearings on Japanese Immigration, 1920, pp. 53-70. Shima had begun with 60 acres of leased land in 1892 and built up his business by 1912 to 1,000 acres of leased land; owner of 400 acres; and leasee of more than 4,600, San Francisco Call, March 10, 1912, p. 6/1.

efforts were highly praised during a produce carnival in Stockton at which he "contributed a display showing his launch--<u>Shima Maru</u> and potato barge, laden with spuds. It won the grand prize and was pronounced one of the finest exhibits of the kind ever seen at a county or state fair."[19]

The following month, the <u>Call</u> took a different view of Shima's success story when potatoes from Dayton, Nevada, were quarantined by the State Horicultural Commission due to infection of the eel worm. The <u>Call</u> pointed out that wholesalers were waiting to see at what price Shima would sell his 900,000 sacks in storage.[20] The cost of a sack of river potatoes was estimated at sixty cents. "If Shima could get a price of $2.50 or $3.00 a sack by a corner [on the market] he stands to make more than one million."[21] Since the new crop of potatoes would not be on the market until May, Shima could maintain his corner on the market for more than three months.

When these "facts" were reported to the San Francisco Labor Council, a committee was appointed to investigate Shima's "corner" on the potato market. The report, submitted to the Council in February, stated that the committee found Shima had been selling his potatoes at "exorbitant" rates. The District Attorney, Mr. Fickert, and federal authorities were consulted by the Labor Council Committee; it concluded that Shima and "his associates could be prosecuted under the state and federal laws and steps would be taken to proceed against them as soon as the necessary affidavits could be secured."[22]

There seems to have been little truth in this "plot" to control the potato market. It should be recalled that the state legislature in January and February of 1911 was engaged in the controversy of the Exclusion League's letter to stop discriminating legislation against Asiatics. The story of Shima's "corner" on the potato market was a special dispatch to the <u>Call</u> from Sacramento[23] and may be considered the newspaper's effort to arouse consumer interests against Japanese farmers and land ownership.

A brief examination of the Call's produce trading and sales column indicates a rise in prices from $1.07 to $1.85 a sack for river white potatoes during the months of February, March, and April.[24] Shima himself denied that he ever had a

---

[19]<u>San Francisco Call</u>, December 16, 1910, p. 18/2. Shima was also highly honored by the College of Agriculture at Berkeley who considered him "one of California's most enlightened agriculturalists ... he has improved the quality of the potatoes grown on the river ranches," <u>San Francisco Call</u>, March 10, 1912, p. 6/1.

[20]The <u>San Francisco Call</u> repeated this distorted figure twice in the January 9 article. On December 16, 1910, p. 18/2, the <u>San Francisco Call</u> wrote: "The potato king has disposed of all his crop, save between 80,000 and 90,000 sacks, and if the market continues to rise, his profits may exceed $200,000."

[21]<u>San Francisco Call</u>, January 9, 1911, p. 4/6.

[22]<u>San Francisco Call</u>, February 5, 1911, p. 34/1.

[23]<u>San Francisco Call</u>, December 16, 1910, p. 18/2; January 9, 1911, p. 4/6.

[24]<u>San Francisco Call</u>, February 5, 1911, p. 50/1; March 28, 1911, p. 15/1; April 12, p. 16/3.

"corner" on the potato market. "It is impossible to do that, there are too many parts of the country that grow good potatoes."[25] The protest of the Call against Shima's success seems to indicate that most growers had few potatoes--mostly poor quality--while Shima had quality and quantity. What he had really cornered was an effective agricultural production technique during a season that, in itself, would have produced a poor crop.

There were other acts of discrimination against Japanese in agricultural areas before 1913. The Board of City Trustees in Vacaville refused to grant a building permit to Japanese contractors to erect the Japanese Methodist Episcopal Church. The trustees believed that the people were determined there should not be a Japanese church within their city.[26] Sutter County fruit growers signed a pact not to pay Japanese more than twelve and a half cents an hour during the fruit season--since the wages to Japanese in former seasons "have been run up during the busiest period to wages equal to those paid to white laborers .... Preference is given to white labor, but a sufficient force of white workers cannot be obtained during the busiest season."[27]

Serious labor trouble was created at Oxnard in 1909 when county officials attempted to collect a local poll tax from 450 Japanese employed in the beet fields. The poll tax caused a great deal of resentment among the Japanese, especially after they had already paid the city tax. It was reported that "the Japanese are moving to other parts of the state, leaving the growers in serious straits for laborers." The Sheriff and County Assessor thought it would be best to recede from their position and return the money and cease the effort to collect any poll tax.[28]

In the Florin area, near Sacramento, the white population became aroused over Japanese acquisition of the largest saloon in town. The Florin Fruit Company, comprised of Japanese and owning several Japanese saloons, was gaining control over the Florin liquor supply. White residents asked the county supervisors to take action against the Japanese. When a petition of thirty-two Japanese was presented at the Florin Fruit Grower's Association asking for membership on the board of directors, the petition was tabled--denying the minority representation on the directorate.[29]

---

[25] San Francisco Call, March 10, 1912, p. 6/2.

[26] San Francisco Bulletin, September 24, 1907, p. 1/3.

[27] San Francisco Call, March 16, 1907, p. 3/1. The Japanese expected to pay board out of their twelve and a half cents an hour wage. There was no agreement entered into regarding the wages paid to white laborers. The situation is ironic when compared to historians such as I. B. Cross and R. D. Hunt, who maintain the stereotype that Japanese cut prices and wages to force out white competition, A History of the Labor Movement in California, p. 264.

[28] San Francisco Call, March 2, 1909, p. 34/4. The tax was two dollars a head and was used to support the public schools. Such an incident as this helped I. B. Cross to build a stereotype against the Japanese: "The Japanese demanded better employment and housing conditions, insisted on controlling the job, violated contracts, struck when the strike would be most inopportune for the farmer ...," I. B. Cross, op. cit., p. 263.

[29] San Francisco Call, March 31, 1911, p. 1/4.

A few miles from Florin, a wealthy Japanese druggist attempted to purchase a home in an exclusive residential section of Sacramento. Described as "a section of beautiful bungalows and pretty cottages," the indignant white residents held a mass meeting to protest the sale by Elmer Truesdale. The Japanese druggist was forced to give up his purchase.[30]

Shortly before the passage of the Alien Land Law, Santa Clara County farmers opened a free employment office in San Jose. Any white man, woman, or child, could register for employment without charge. Under the leadership of C. H. Dement, the employment office was financed by the co-operative Farmer's Education Union "which for several years past had been doing its best to displace the Japanese in the fruit picking industry."[31]

As a result of discrimination, Japanese had to form their own social or professional organization such as the Japanese Association of America; the Japanese Association of American College Graduates; the Japanese Dental Society of California; the Japanese Laundry Association; and the Japanese Business Men's Club.[32] These groups promoted social relations among the Japanese population.

Social discrimination of Japanese in business and labor was to have a profound effect in the public schools. Certain politicians knew they could win public support as well as influence and prestige from the newspapers if they intimated problems of racial miscegenation. Legislators played upon this theme of racial intermixture in the public schools by introducing discriminating legislation to segregate certain minorities into separate schools. The protection of school children, especially girls--"innocent white maids" from immoral, lecherous immigrants became a myth propounded by certain exclusionists in the legislature.

The legislative sessions of 1907, 1909, and 1911 contained not only alien land bills, but segregation bills to remove Japanese from public schools. All of these bills, up until the passage of the Alien Land Law of 1913, were stopped by the

---

[30] San Francisco Call, February 6, 1912, p. 5/4.

[31] San Francisco Call, July 24, 1912, p. 15/6. This paper encouraged the farmer's efforts to reduce Asiatic farm laborers by increasing the employment of school children, San Francisco Call, November 22, 1910, p. 6/1; February 23, 1911, p. 6/1.

[32] San Francisco Call, February 26, 1907, p. 14/4. Apparently, citizenship was not a qualification for admittance to the Federal and State Bar Examination. The San Francisco Call stated that Masuji Miyakawa, a correspondent of a local Japanese paper, was the first and only Japanese lawyer admitted to the Federal and State Bars, San Francisco Call, February 3, 1907, p. 24/4. The San Francisco Chronicle, beginning in January 1915, published annually materials paid by Japanese individuals to counter the anti-Japanese stereotype built up by the news media. The material published by prominent Japanese indicates that their clientele was primarily Japanese. Elliot Mears states that the United States Immigration Commissioner's report of 1910 is "not strictly true" in stating that Chinese and Japanese were not allowed to become members of fraternal organizations in America. Mears lists the Masons, Knights of Columbus, Rotary International, and Kiwanis--all of whom are primarily professional men's clubs. The ones who discriminated were the middle class social-interest type groups, cf. E. G. Mears, Resident Orientals on the American Pacific Coast, p. 163.

Governor--sometimes with recommendations from the President. The school bills were generally considered by some newspapers to be "cheap politics" created by political mountebanks who played to the galleries.[33]

The decision to segregate Japanese in San Francisco public schools on October 11, 1906, was to precipitate what became the "White Maid of California" myth. The Board of Education adopted the following resolution:

> Resolved: That in accordance with Article 1, section 1662 of the school law of California, principals are hereby directed to send all Chinese, Japanese, and Korean children to the Oriental Public School, situated on the south side of Clay Street, on and after October 15, 1906.[34]

The action of the board was firmly denounced by the President of the Japanese Association of America, K. Kadico, who stated that appeal would be made to the Federal Courts on the grounds of discrimination against a class of persons on the basis of race or color.[35] Such a view was ignored by the politicians--such as Senator Frank McGowan who spoke at a mass anti-Japanese rally in December 1906. "He made a strong appeal to preserve the American public schools from Asiatics. 'The sacred confines of the public school, while God gives us sight, shall never be contaminated.'"[36] The Senator's idea was again reflected by San Francisco Attorney Burke who stated, "A deep principle is here involved--the protection of our little ones from the contaminating influences of a low class of foreigners who are continually coming to our shores."[37] Governor Pardee, in an open letter to Theodore Roosevelt, put the school problem on a less emotional basis.

> Many of the Japanese who desire to attend our schools are much older than the Caucasian children with whom, on account of their deficient learning, the Japanese must be enclosed. It is not at all desirable that youths, even Caucasian [sic] youths, of eighteen or more of age should be associated in the schools with children of tender ages.[38]

---

[33] San Francisco Call, February 10, 1909, p. 2/1. David S. Jordan thought that those leaders in the 1909 legislature who favored anti-Japanese legislation "were playing to the gallery and were misinformed." However, he thought A. M. Drew was sincere in his advocacy of an anti-alien land law.

[34] San Francisco Call, December 8, 1906, p. 5/4.

[35] San Francisco Call, October 26, 1906, p. 5/2.

[36] San Francisco Call, December 24, 1906, p. 2/2.

[37] San Francisco Call, January 18, 1907, p. 16/5.

[38] San Francisco Call, January 9, 1907, p. 5/2. A little over a week later a meeting was held at the Unitarian Club. In attendance was David S. Jordan, George Kennan, "the Yankee of the Orient" and John Irish who read a communication from a principal of a local school, who declared that the Japanese pupils excelled the American students. The principal desired to remain anonymous. San Francisco Call, January 18, 1907, p. 16/5.

The school board rescinded the exclusion order on March 13, 1907, but not before Senator Wolfe of San Francisco succeeded in having his bill approved in the Senate to "prohibit children over ten years old from enter primary schools."[39] This bill was not needed, for the following day School Super endent Roncovieri returned from the conference in Washington and announce1 that.

> the number of Japanese school children in S 1 Francisco under the terms of the agreement reached would l insignificant. According to [Roncovieri's] statement ther are but 93 Japanese pupils in the city, of whom all but 45 will be barred from the schools because they are more than 16 years old. The examinations, he said, would reduce the number of eligibles to 12 or 15 and these would be principally pupils in the primary grades.[40]

The theory or the "protection" of white children by segregation was raised again in the 1909 Legislature on January 22 when Grove L. Johnson introduced a school bill to extend and strengthen the provisions of the state law under which the San Francisco Board of Education had attempted to segregate the Japanese in 1906.[41] When Johnson introduced his bill, he blatantly stated:

> I know more about the Japanese than Governor Gillett and President Roosevelt put together. I am not responsible to either of them. I am responsible to the Mothers and Fathers of Sacramento County who have their little daughters sitting side by side in the school rooms with matured Japs, with their base minds, their lascivious thoughts multiplied by their race and strengthened by their mode of life. I am here to protect the children of these parents and to do all that I can to keep any Asiatic man from mingling in the same school

---

[39] San Francisco Call, March 9, 1907, p. 2/4. Cf. Bailey, op. cit., p. 176. The San Francisco Call reported that Japanese would soon be "taking advantage of the open school doors and the protection afforded them by the big stick," San Francisco Call, March 15, 1907, p. 2/3. Senator Edward Wolfe stated at one of the Asiatic Exclusion League meetings: "I am heartily in favor of excluding the Japanese and always have been. My record shows that I am for union labor always," San Francisco Call, March 21, 1910, p. 5/1.

[40] San Francisco Call, March 10, 1907, p. 33/2. Dr. H. B. Johnson testified in 1920 that "one of the leading papers stated that there were 2,000 children of Japanese parentage in the public schools, and a large proportion of them were adolescent. I knew that to be false and made a public statement the next day to the effect that there were less than 100 Japanese children ... 86, as I remember now, and that they were scattered in 23 different schools in San Francisco." Hearings on Japanese Immigration, 1920, p. 584.

[41] Assembly Journal, 1909, p. 222. Cf. also Bailey, op. cit., p. 307. Johnson introduced two bills in 1909: AB 14, "Asiatic School Bill" and AB 32, "Municipal Segregation Bill" both of which were reconsidered and withdrawn. Hichborn, Legislation of 1909, p. 201; Appendix, p. xxxii-xxxiii.

with the daughters of our people. You know the results of such
a condition; you know how far it will go, and I have seen
Japanese 25 years old sitting in the seats next to the pure
maids of California. I shudder to think of such a condition.[42]

When Johnson's anti-Japanese school bill passed the Assembly on February 4,
1909, by a vote of 45 to 29,[43] the editor of the Call denounced the action.

> When the people of this state see a measure of this character
> propounded by a mischievous political mountebank like Grove
> Johnson they consider the source and pay small attention, but
> in the East they know Johnson only as a member of the legislature
> and do not understand that he is either playing to the gallery or
> working for some hidden personal advantage.[44]

Governor Gillette, who wanted to avoid discriminatory legislation, joined
President Roosevelt's efforts to modify an embarrassing situation. The Governor
questioned the extent of Japanese population in the public schools.[45] The statistical information compiled by the Governor revealed that Japanese school children
in the major cities amounted to 573. San Francisco had 128; Los Angeles, 128;
Oakland, 80; Sacramento, 54; Berkeley, 32; San Jose, 32; Fresno, 31; Alameda, 30;
Santa Cruz, 15; Salinas, 14; San Diego, 6; Santa Barbara, 6; Bakersfield, 6;
Stockton, 5; Santa Rosa, 4; San Bernardino, 1; and Chico, 1.[46] The Governor's
statistics illustrated the relatively small number of Japanese in the public schools
of the urban areas. Other information indicates there were 817 Japanese children
in the state's public schools in 1909 with the following grade distribution:

	Male	Female
Kindergarten	1	5
Primary schools	269	149
Grammar schools	150	31
High schools	137	3
Evening schools	71	1
Totals	628	189[47]

---

[42]Hichborn, Legislature of 1909, p. 207; Daniels, op. cit., pp. 47-48. The Asiatic
Exclusion League encouraged Johnson to stand pat on his anti-Japanese bills. San
Francisco Call, January 29, 1909, p. 4/4.

[43]Ibid., p. 208; Bailey, op. cit., p. 309. The Asiatic Exclusion League later
claimed that Johnson's school segregation bill would have passed 42 to 36 if all
the legislators had voted as they promised "and our little daughters would not,
as they are now, be sitting side by side in the schoolroom with mature Japanese
of base minds." San Francisco Call, May 28, 1910, p. 5/4.

[44]San Francisco Call, February 4, 1909, p. 6/2. Johnson's previous actions were not
consistently anti-Japanese. When the Drew Bill to limit land owned by aliens
passed the Assembly in 1907, Johnson stood alone as the one dissenting vote. San
Francisco Call, March 1, 1907, p. 3/1. He reversed his opposition to an alien land
law in 1913: "For my part I do not believe that the passage of this bill will
hurt the Exposition to the extent of fifteen cents." Sacramento Bee, April 3,
1913, p. 5/1. Cf. also Kessler, op. cit., p. 111.

[45]San Francisco Call, February 9, 1909, p. 2/2. Will C. Wood, School Superintendent,
reported there were 30 Japanese attending the schools in Alameda and that the
number was constantly increasing. At Berkeley, Frank F. Bunker reported that 32
Japanese students were present in a school census of 6,000.

By the end of 1912, the Japanese school population had increased to the following proportions:

Primary and grammar schools, public	1,183
High school, public	139
Colleges and universities	105
Japanese kindergarten and primary schools, private	678
"Special" schools for adults, Japanese, private	570
Totals	2,675[48]

Even with the publication of figures on the number of Japanese students in the public schools, along with the Governor's opposition, school bills were again introduced in the 1911 legislature. On January 16, Assemblyman Fred H. Hall, referred to as the champion of the "Pink Cheeked Girl of the Golden West,"[49] introduced AB 486:

> providing for separate schools for Indian, Mongolian, Chinese, Japanese, Malay, and Hindoo [sic] children; excluding adult Indian, Chinese, Mongolian, Malays, Japanese, and Hindoos [sic] from the public schools of the state, and authorizing the exclusion of children of filthy or vicious habits.[50]

A Japanese school exclusion bill was introduced in the 1913 legislature, but like its predecessors, it was not passed; probably because the alien land issue had become a major concern.[51] However, the "White Maid" or "Pink Cheeked Girl" myths did not disappear because it was not written into law--it became legend[52]

---

[46] San Francisco Call, February 17, 1909, p. 2/4.

[47] San Francisco Call, May 30, 1910, p. 2/5.

[48] San Francisco Call, May 4, 1913, p. 24/1. The published information was Japanese advertisement quoting United States Immigration Commissioner's report for 1912, XXIII, pp. 159-160.

[49] San Francisco Chronicle, January 17, 1911, p. 2/1. The paper stated that it shall be the duty of the governing body of each school district of the state to establish separate schools if possible; otherwise, separate buildings should be secured to separate the white children from all others. In April, the board of directors of Stockton public schools petitioned to sell part of Franklin School grounds to purchase a new school site. "It is stated further that the board intends using the Franklin School for Japanese, Chinese, and Negroes only," San Francisco Call, April 25, 1911, p. 5/2.

[50] Assembly Journal, 1911, p. 185. Cf. Kessler, op. cit., p. 15. The bill was referred to the Committee on Education and was not reported out of committee, Assembly Journal, 1911, p. 2671. The delegate from the Asiatic Exclusion League at the State Building Trades Council at San Rafael recommended that "aliens be prohibited from holding land and be separated from white children in the public schools," San Francisco Call, January 20, 1911, p. 3/1.

[51] S.B. 1285 was intended to define the problem of including Japanese under the term "Mongolian" as stated in Article I, Section 1662 of the school law of California. Cf. Kessler, op. cit., p. 87.

[52] Some individuals believed the legend could be proven true if the issue could be put on a ballot. W. R. Jacobs, an attorney, landowner, and resident of Stockton, testified on July 16, 1920: "The feeling that existed at that time [during the San Francisco School incident, 1906-1907] exists today, and if a referendum were to be taken in Stockton upon the question of the social assimilation of the Japanese boys and the white girls there would be a vote against it of 95 percent." Hearings on Japanese Immigration, 1920, p. 523.

propounded by the members of the Oriental Exclusion League formed in 1919 under the leadership of the State Controller, John S. Chambers[53] and V. S. McClatchy, part owner of the Bee.

J. M. Inman, State Senator from Sacramento, and President of the Oriental Exclusion League in 1919, again raised the legend of the "White Maid" before the Native Sons and Daughters of the Golden West:

> The Placer County school census for 1919 showed more than 10 percent of all children to be Japanese. One school in that county shows that there are seventeen pupils; thirteen are Japanese. And in this school there is one little white girl. Would that some of those that believe that all men are born equal had fathered this little girl![54]

During the hearings on Japanese immigration on March 13, 1924, shortly before the Japanese were excluded on a racial basis, James D. Phelan, one of the most persistent anti-Japanese politicians on the Pacific slope,[55] again enunciated the "White Maid" myth:

> The farmers and the other people of the country did not like their little girls sitting side by side with these Japs. Bear in mind that the Japanese 'school boy' was often one of the big fellows who came over densely ignorant, but of mature age. They would be in those school rooms with the little girls, and the

---

[53] In a speech before the San Luis Obispo Chamber of Commerce, Chambers claimed that Japanese adults in many rural communities were "crowding little American children from American schools." San Francisco Examiner, September 17, 1920, p. 10/1.

[54] J. M. Inman, "The Time Has Arrived to Eliminate the Japs as California Landholders," Grizzly Bear, XXVII (June 1920), p. 5. Cf. the repetition of Inman's statements by Mrs. Cora M. Woodbridge, wife of the Mayor of Roseville, and a member of the Oriental Exclusion League in Hearings on Japanese Immigration, 1920, pp. 284-287.

[55] Daniels believes that "Phelan was the only anti-Japanese political leader in California before the First World War to subscribe to the Yellow Peril." Daniels, op. cit., pp. 70-71. Theodore A. Bell, who opposed Hiram Johnson for the governor's office in 1910, stated in his campaign: "The races of Asia, whose naturalization is impossible, should never be allowed to gain a foothold on our soil. I believe that the Federal Government should forbid Asiatic Immigration of any character, but in the absence of the nation's acting in the matter, I believe that our State should exercise all its reserve powers to protect itself against the evils of Asiatic immigration." Sacramento Bee, September 7, 1910, p. 12/1. Dr. Rockwell Dennis Hunt, perhaps as much of a white racist as Phelan in that both believed California should be preserved and protected for the white race, wrote: "We may say of James Phelan that it was his human side that will be best and most gratefully remembered ... as a Christian he was sincere, self-forgetting, and faithful .... His life was spent in a worthy endeavor to make his California better." R. D. Hunt, California's Stately Hall of Fame, 1950, p. 482.

> Japanese, notoriously, are unmoral people. In matters of that
> kind they are an extreme danger, and I have very good authority
> for what I say.[56]

Such emotional propaganda most certainly had its effect on the voting population as well as the nation's representatives, but there seems to have been little grounds for the charge that the Japanese were an immoral people.[57] Although not stated openly, what is implied in these "White Maid" statements is a fear of racial miscegenation, a factor that could rally any white community into a substantially organized opposition to a racial minority such as the Japanese. Another factor which may be inferred from these statements is a kind of jealousy of the mature Japanese who wanted an education in American customs and standards so badly, he was willing to associate with children to attain Americanization. It may have been this social drive for an equal education in American public schools which eventually gained an equal status for Japanese in American society by the 1950's.

---

[56] *Japanese Immigration Legislature: Hearings on SB 2576*, March 11-13, 15, 1924, 60th Congress, 1st Session, p. 111. Phelan was undoubtedly responsible for injecting into the 1912 State Democratic Campaign that Roosevelt believed "grown Japanese men should be allowed to mingle in the public schools with white boys and girls of tender years!" R. L. Buell, "The Development of Anti-Japanese Agitation in the United States, II," p. 60.

[57] Cf. W. G. Beach, Oriental Crime in California, a sociological-statistical study of Japanese and Chinese crime rates in California from 1900-1930. The author's conclusion is that Orientals during the first quarter of the Twentieth Century have a very low crime rate compared to their population. The Japanese are especially shown to be a highly moral and conforming social group to American middle class standards.

CHAPTER V

THE POLITICS OF NATIVISM--1907-1912

This point above all I wish to emphasize: the unAmerican attitude of the California newspapers. The Los Angeles papers always have printed but one side of the question. The many fine points brought out at the recent investigations favoring the Japanese were almost entirely ignored by the daily papers. Without great expense the voter cannot be reached except by the newspapers.

>Sworn testimony of Mrs. Bertha E. Kori, American wife of a Japanese, Los Angeles, July 20, 1920, before the House Immigration and Naturalization Committee, <u>Japanese Immigration Hearings</u>, p. 1017.

CHAPTER V

THE POLITICS OF NATIVISM--1907-1912

Although there was economic, social, and political discrimination against the Japanese, legal discrimination had to be couched in legally accepted terminology. To achieve this, the politicians based their actions on the statutes dealing with naturalization and eligibility to citizenship. Again, the labor unions provided the impetus for the politicians. One of the easiest ways to discriminate, without openly naming a particular race, was to make the basis of membership dependent upon citizenship. The union labor view was well stated by Tveitmoe at a mass rally on Japanese immigration.

> A Chinese or a Japanese is a Chinese or a Japanese always. You could not make a citizen out of him if you swore him on a stack of Bibles as high as the Washington Monument. He would always turn his gun against the white man, for he believed his Mikado to be a god and would be willing to die for him if he had a thousand lives .... Mongolians believe they have a civilization superior to that of the white races and they do not desire to be made Americans.[1]

The most representative voice among politicians on the Japanese Naturalization issue was James D. Phelan. For better than fifty years Phelan maintained one view on Naturalization: "Our government is one of white men ... the Japanese is not desirable as a citizen; in fact, he is unassimilable."[2] As the leading Democrat in California, it was James D. Phelan who made Japanese Naturalization an issue in the 1912 presidential campaign. Phelan wrote an anti-Oriental tract and then had the presidential aspirant, Woodrow Wilson, issue the statement as his own on May 3, 1912.[3] The literature was distributed on a car--representing Wilson to be the champion of Asiatic exclusion on one side, while Theodore Roosevelt was quoted as an advocate of Japanese naturalization on the other side.[4] The Progressive-Republican view of the Democratic anti-Oriental propaganda was to have a profound effect in the 1913 legislature. Governor Johnson estimated that the Progressive ticket lost, conservatively, 10,000 votes as a result of the card's dissemination.[5]

---

[1] *San Francisco Call*, December 24, 1906, p. 2/2.

[2] *San Francisco Call*, January 22, 1907, p. 2/3. Phelan began his political concern in the 1800's and continued his anti-Oriental views until his death in the 1930's. See James D. Phelan, "Letter on the Chinese Question," *Overland Monthly*, M.S. VII (March 1886), p. 328ff.

[3] Robert E. Hennings, "James D. Phelan and the Woodrow Wilson Anti-Oriental Statement of May 3, 1912," *California Historical Society Quarterly*, XXXII (December 1963), p. 291.

[4] The contents of the statement may be found in: Hennings, op. cit., pp. 293-295; J. O. Davis to Joseph P. Tumulty, January 4, 1913, State Department Paper, 811.52/34, cited in Kessler, *The Political Factors in California's Anti-Alien Land Legislation, 1912-1913*, p. 55; Hichborn, *Legislature of 1913*, pp. 213-214; Johnson MSS, Part One, Box 37, cited in Daniels, op. cit., p. 134.

[5] Letter, Hiram Johnson to Theodore Roosevelt, June 21, 1913, Johnson Papers, cited in Kessler, op. cit., p. 56. Johnson may have picked up this idea from a statement

There appeared to be little consistency in lower court decisions on Japanese naturalization before the passage of the Alien Land Law of 1913. The whole matter of racial origin, both geographic and social, had not been defined by the court system so that some Japanese had been naturalized before the Supreme Court in 1922 finally determined the ineligibility of Japanese for naturalization. Supreme Court Judge, Justice B. Sutherland, in the Ozawa Case [260 U.S. 178 (1922)] held that Takao Ozawa was ineligible to citizenship by reason of his race. Sutherland based his decision on Section 2169 in Title XXX of the Revised Statutes on naturalization which stated, in part: "The provisions of this title shall apply to aliens being free white persons and to aliens of African nativity and to persons of African descent."[6]

A Japanese citizen, Alfred E. Tatsumi, had been naturalized by Judge Hebbard in 1897. Unfortunately, his papers were destroyed in the San Francisco fire of 1906. When he applied for restoration of his papers, Superior Court Judge Graham refused renewal "on the grounds that a Japanese is a Mongolian and therefore not eligible to citizenship in the United States."[7] The judge based his decision on a judgment rendered in the Supreme Court of Massachusetts against a Japanese named Saito.[8]

During May and June 1907, the Call carried a series of articles on a naturalization case in Los Angeles. Announced as the "first formal petition for naturalization of a Japanese ever received at the office of the Los Angeles County Clerk,"[9] the District Attorney believed that two Japanese photographers, Joseph Fetsuo Wada and Moni Suski, could become citizens due to changes in the naturalization laws made by Congress in 1906. The county clerk was instructed to hold all further proceedings until a decision of the federal authorities at Washington could make an investigation.[10] Within a week, the Los Angeles County Clerk received an answer from the chief of the division of Naturalization whose opinion was that the county clerk

---

made by Senator Frank Smith: "If Theodore Roosevelt hadn't come here several years ago with a big stick, he would have carried the state of California by 100,000 majority." San Francisco Call, May 4, 1913, p. 19/3.

[6]John B. Trevor, Japanese Exclusion, a Study of the Policy and the Law, p. 58.

[7]San Francisco Call, October 26, 1906, p. 5/2. Some Japanese contented they were Malaya and Aryan in lineage, and might fairly claim to be classified ethnologically as the white persons described in the naturalization act. San Francisco Call, April 15, 1913, p. 2/4.

[8]Ibid. The Call later contained an editorial on a Japanese who was denied naturalization in a Federal Court in Chicago. Judge Carter based his decision on the naturalization statute section 2169, that limits naturalization to any free white man or persons of African descent. He pointed out that the statute applies to Mongolians "and a Japanese is surely a Mongolian." San Francisco Call, December 18, 1906, p. 8/1.

[9]San Francisco Call, May 16, 1907, p. 5/5. In the succeeding article it was stated that the application of the two Japanese was "the first application of the kind ever accepted in this country." San Francisco Call, May 24, 1907, p. 5/4.

[10]San Francisco Call, May 24, 1907, p. 5/4.

would "have no legal right to accept such declarations from Japanese because subjects of the Mikado are not eligible to citizenship."[11] The only alternative left for the Japanese was to announce they would seek to compel the county clerk to issue naturalization papers by instituting Mandamus proceedings in the United States Courts to test the ruling. It was decided, perhaps for financial reasons, to abandon the Mandamus proceedings "without further contest to the ruling of the Department of Immigration."[12]

The issue of Japanese naturalization again became of paramount importance with the passage of the alien land law in 1913 since the law made no specific reference to Japanese as such, but only to those "ineligible to citizenship." California legislators, many of whom were lawyers, knew that most court decisions had held that Japanese were not eligible to naturalization.[13] They also knew that Article I, Section seventeen of the State Constitution left "to the legislature the power to forbid the taking or holding of property by aliens ineligible to citizenship within the state's limits."[14]

The Alien Land Law of 1913 was the end result of a battle between Democrats and Republicans in the previous three legislative sessions. The concept of an alien land law, however, had its origins in the Chinese exclusion movement of the 1880's. The Workingman's Party and the Grange allied themselves to discuss proposed constitutional provisions before the State Constitutional Convention assembled at Sacramento during September 1878. They introduced proposals that were not only unsuccessful, but extremely radical at the time. Among these were the following: "No Mongolian to be hired by any corporation; aliens not to be permitted to own, sell, or acquire by any means, any interest in real estate in California; no person to be permitted to settle in California if unable to become a citizen of the State."[15]

The first alien land bill was presented in the Assembly by A. M. Drew of Fresno.[16] The bill provided that no alien could hold title to real property for more than five years and forbade leases to aliens for more than a year. The bill passed the Assembly on March 1, 1907, with only one dissenting vote--Grove Johnson. Drew pointed out the cause for presenting his alien land bill--"one third of the [land] titles passed in Fresno County last year [1906] went to Japanese."[17] None

---

[11] San Francisco Call, June 1, 1907, p. 3/3. The decision from Washington was based on section 2169, Revised Statutes. It was this statute which finally denied Ozawa citizenship.

[12] San Francisco Call, June 12, 1907, p. 10/2.

[13] San Francisco Call, April 15, 1913, p. 2/4.

[14] Ex Parte Y. Akado (1912), 207.P.245, 188c. 739. Cited in West's Annotated California Codes (St. Paul, Minnesota, 1954), p. 526.

[15] I. B. Cross, A History Of The Labor Movement in California, p. 117. Cross had some strong ideas about immigration himself: "We oppose the immigration of any race, no matter what its virtues, that comes to us in any large numbers. We truly need a modern Moses to lead us out of this Wilderness of Confusion," San Francisco Examiner, August 10, 1915, p. 5/1. The exclusion movement was to find its "Moses" in the person of V. S. McClatchy.

[16] Hichborn, Legislature of 1909, p. 203.

[17] San Francisco Call, March 1, 1907, p. 3/1. Anti-Oriental and anti-Japanese bills were presented by Senators Caminetti and Sanford, but none of them were successful, Buell, "The Development of Anti-Japanese Agitation in the United States, I," p. 630.

of the discriminating bills in the 1907 Legislature were written into law, but certain legislators thought the Governor and the President were "misguided" in their attempt to protect the Japanese minority.[18] When Roosevelt had suggested to Congress that discrimination would be reduced if an act were passed to naturalize Japanese, one of the "Hottentots" for the California Senate, J. B. Sanford, drew up a joint resolution condemning the President for urging the naturalization of "a race that cannot be assimilated by the Caucasian race."[19]

Between the two legislative sessions of 1907 and 1909, the newspapers of San Francisco engaged in a rabid campaign to create public interest in the Anti-Japanese movement by spreading the fear of war and a racial invasion from Japan. Even before the legislature had adjourned in 1907, the editor of the Call stated:

> What the Pacific Coast wants is exclusion that will exclude--exclusion by law and not by treaty; exclusion clothed with force of a federal statute and not a mere regulation dependent upon the judgment of any man, wise or unwise, President or plain citizen. Mayor Schmitz would better not bring home any other kind of a bargain .... They [Japanese] are taking away the cut-flower industry from the Italians and Portuguese, and they are making a beginning on fruit drying. In fact, they have taken complete possession of certain important fruit-growing districts in this State, with the result that American families have left those neighborhoods.[20]

The Call published articles on what it called "a war of races" in the Imperial Valley. Mexicans and Indians had been employed as manual labor on the railroads and in the irrigation ditches. The arrival of large numbers of Japanese reduced the wage rate with the result of warnings being issued by the Mexican and Indian population that "the valley is entirely too small to hold them [Japanese], and that they better get out."[21]

---

[18] On February 1, Governor Gillett published a telegram from the California delegation in Washington, asking that the legislature "defer all action concerning Japanese," San Francisco Call, February 1, 1907, p. 2/4.

[19] San Francisco Call, January 12, 1907, p. 3/6; Buell, "The Development of Anti-Japanese Agitation in the United States, I," p. 630. Sanford, a controversial figure in the Senate, was not well liked by Governor Johnson. Will H. Fischer, editor of The California Outlook in 1913, characterized Sanford as follows: "The four-flusher dotes on front, banks on noise, lives on publicity, and shirks on work ... 'The gray eagle of Mendocino' the Hearst papers call him ..." Fischer, "Sanford of Ukiah," The California Outlook, XIV (February 1, 1913), p. 5, cited in Kessler, op. cit., p. 74, note 20.

[20] San Francisco Call, February 15, 1907, p. 6/1. Cf. also the editorials on June 13, 1907, p. 8/1 and June 15, 1907, p. 8/1. On June 15, under the title "Japanese Monkeyshines," the editor stated: "There is one inexorable conclusion enforced by these occurrences, and it is that the Japanese are undesirable neighbors. They are trouble breeders and their presence in this country is a constant menace."

[21] San Francisco Call, June 11, 1907, p. 3/7.

A second, and more convincing myth circulated by the politicians and the newspapers was the "land myth" which became more formalized after the introduction of the alien land laws in the 1907 legislature. Quoting the Turlock Journal on the establishment of a large Japanese colony in the San Joaquin Valley, the Call editor warned:

> This Japanese colony will develop their land to the highest extent and have already begun preparing it for fruits, vines and gardens. These wily fellows will have a little Japan right in the midst of the whites, and the experience of the Americans at Vacaville and other points in California where the brown men have settled thickly is likely to be repeated .... The white settlers on the outskirts of the Japanese colony will find the neighborhood undesirable and their land depreciated by Japanese. The process is capable of indefinite repetition and expansion, and if the Japanese are permitted to come here in large numbers, it is inevitable.[22]

Not all of the farmers in the state joined with the politicians and newspapers in their propaganda against the Japanese. Fruit growers of the Sacramento Valley sent a petition to Congress and the President demanding the admission of Asiatic labor and enterprise to California under no other restrictions than are imposed upon the admission of European labor and enterprise on the Atlantic Coast. The petition concludes: "To save California from the decadence of her industries with reference to the soil, we demand the admission to our state of Japanese free labor."[23] The New York Sun was later quoted in the Call with reference to the fruit growers resolution:

> Representatives Hayes and Kahn perhaps cannot avoid introducing their Japanese exclusion bills, unless they are prepared to return to private life, but this resolution of the fruit growers has lighted in their rear a fire which mere rhetoric cannot put out.[24]

---

[22] San Francisco Call, September 29, 1907, p. 24/1. This same myth was circulated with increased intensity and slight variations. Cf. Lyman Abbott, "The Alien Land Bill in California," The Outlook CIV (April 19, 1913), p. 828.
L. Abbott, "Japanese in California: A Poll of the Press," The Outlook CIV (May 3, 1913), p. 23.
Percy Edwards, "The Industrial Side of the Alien Land Law Problem," The Overland Monthly, LXII (August 1913), p. 190.
James D. Phelan, "The Japanese Question from a Californian Standpoint," The Independent, LXXIV (June 26, 1913), p. 1,439.
H. A. Millis, "California and the Japanese," The Survey, XXX (June 1913), p. 336.
A. E. Yoell, "Oriental vs. American Labor," Annals of the American Academy of Social and Political Science, XXXIV (September 1909), p. 254.
Chester H. Rowell, "Orientophobia," Collier's Weekly, reprinted in San Francisco Call, February 14, 1909, p. 28/3-6.
Cross, op. cit., pp. 263-264.

[23] San Francisco Call, August 3, 1907, p. 2/3.

[24] San Francisco Call, December 17, 1907, p. 6/1.

The Call claimed an agent of the Pacific Mail Steamship Company lobbied the resolution through the fruit growers' convention.

> Those resolutions do not represent California opinion. They
> have been repudiated in every part of the state, and the fact
> that the New York Sun takes them as gospel is further proof
> that they represent nothing but the sentiment of certain
> powerful corporations that want cheap labor, even at the cost
> of lowering the American standard of living.[25]

The Chambers of Commerce of San Francisco and Los Angeles joined the effort, along with valley fruit growers, to condemn anti-Japanese agitation in the San Francisco Press. On a number of occasions, the San Francisco Chamber of Commerce, Mayor E. R. Taylor, and K. Abiko, President of the Japanese Association worked together to build a more cordial environment between Japan and the United States.[26]

The anti-Japanese press of San Francisco was noticed in other parts of the world, as well. The Call quoted the London Times that racial distrust and hatred were being fanned in every possible way because the whites were confronted with a civilization more efficient than the American. The Call retorted that Japanese "could not compete for an instant with the poorest class of white labor at even wages. Besides their inferiority as laborers, they are tricky and untrustworthy. The 'Yellow Peril' exists because cheap labor threatens the American standard of living."[27]

The San Francisco press found it convenient to keep an aroused public interest in Japanese problems by frequent allusions to war and threats of invasion from Japan. What was called "the first Japanese convention in America" was held in Penryn and attended by five hundred Japanese to take action on the "exclusion act." The Call reported that many were willing to leave California at once to prepare for a fight against the United States.[28] The following day the Call published an article datelined Berlin, under the title "Says Japanese Would Find Coast Vulnerable." California was pointed out as offering an excellent chance of success for an invading Japanese Navy. It was declared that "Japan is working feverishly to complete her military and naval equipment ... during the last few months 50,000 men have been at work day and night in the arsenals turning out guns and small arms."[29]

On November 8, the Call gave front page coverage to an article written by R. O. Matheson under the title "Japanese in Hawaii offer Services to Emperor; Utmost Secrecy Attends Action of Aliens; Believe that War With This Country is at

---

[25]Ibid.

[26]San Francisco Call, August 18, 1907, p. 29/5; June 16, 1909, p. 4/4; September 23, 1910, p. 16/7. The San Francisco Chamber of Commerce opposed both the 1913 and 1920 Alien Land Laws. The Los Angeles Chamber of Commerce, as early as 1905, opposed the anti-Japanese press in San Francisco. Matson, The Anti-Japanese Movement in California, 1890-1942, p. 70.

[27]San Francisco Call, January 16, 1908, p. 6/1.

[28]San Francisco Call, March 15, 1907, p. 2/4.

[29]San Francisco Call, March 16, 1907, p. 2/3.

Hand." Matheson's conclusion was that in the event of any clash between the United States and Japan, the Japanese in Hawaii would work as a unit to give loyal support to the Emperor. "Every subject of the Oriental monarch living here is firmly of the belief that such a conflict is Near."[30] Four days later the Call published the response of the Japanese Ambassador to the propaganda and relegated the information to page nine. The ambassador regretted the interpretation of a passage in the Imperial Rescript on Education, issued on October 30, 1890, and read each year on certain festival occasions which admonished subjects of Japan to offer themselves to the state in cases of emergency. The ambassador stated that the press had erroneously concluded the passage was a special message from the Emperor.[31]

Supreme Court Justice Harlan spoke at the annual dinner of the Navy League on a great future conflict between the yellow and white races. "If it comes, I want to see our country in a position to meet it .... If I had the opportunity, I would vote for an appropriation of $50,000,000 for a period of ten years for a larger Navy."[32] The State Building Trades Council not only passed its usual resolution urging exclusion of Asiatics, but passed a resolution by O. A. Tveitmoe "for more modern battleships, fortifications for the Pacific Coast, a Naval base for San Francisco, and a breakwater at Monterey."[33]

The Call and Examiner on January 16 and 17, 1908, engaged in a bit of yellow journalism over the war scare. On January 16, the Examiner published a map of San Francisco and Marin County fortification positions. The following day, the Call reproduced the Examiner map under the title, "An American Paper for the Japanese People."[34] The editor of the Call denounced the Examiner as "Traitor or Liar-- which?"

> The Examiner of this city prints an elaborate map of the fortifications designed for the protection of San Francisco ....
> Now if these are secret plans of the government, it is treason to publish them .... As if proud of its treachery, the Examiner emphasizes the secrecy of government military preparations, which the paper takes elaborate pains to expose and nullify ....
> Mr. Hearst presents himself in the light of one who would sell his country's secrets for five cents. This is the person who has incorporated a privately owned political party to run him for President of the United States.[35]

---

[30] San Francisco Call, November 8, 1907, p. 1/7 and p. 2/2.
[31] San Francisco Call, November 12, 1907, p. 9/7.
[32] San Francisco Call, January 12, 1908, p. 40/4.
[33] San Francisco Call, January 17, 1908, p. 7/3.
[34] San Francisco Call, January 17, 1908, p. 2/1-3.
[35] San Francisco Call, January 18, 1908, p. 6/2. The political cartoon in this issue, entitled "Jap and me" shows W. R. Hearst seated in the middle of a bowed slat stretched across a slough. To Hearst's right is a cage with a bee inside. The cage is tagged "Presidential Bee." Hearsts' left hand is wrapped around a Japanese naval officer while they both look over maps spread out before them with titles of "Plans for U.S. Fortification." A little over three years later, the Call published an article on the installation of five search lights able to throw a ray of light eight miles. "Their rays of light will enable the gunners to direct the fire of the big guns [at the Presidio] against a hostile fleet in case of war," San Francisco Call, March 21, 1911, p. 16/5.

While the newspapers continued increasingly to agitate for exclusion of Japanese immigration, the California Legislature of 1909 introduced some seventeen measures directed at the Japanese.[36] In the Assembly, Grove Johnson presented bills 14, 15, and 32; while A. M. Drew presented bill 78 to prevent aliens from holding title to real estate. In the Senate, J. B. Sanford introduced bill 71--drawn along the same general lines as the Drew bill.[37] The Assembly bill provided that an alien acquiring title to land within the state would have to become a citizen within five years or dispose of his holdings. Even though the Japanese were not mentioned, their ineligibility to citizenship made the bill discriminatory legislation. The agitation was brought to a head on January 15, 1909, when the Assembly Judiciary Committee reported favorably Drew's Alien land bill.[38]

Again, as in the 1907 Legislature, President Roosevelt used the "big stick" to stop discriminating legislation. The President insisted there was no need for new laws to regulate the Japanese whose rights were guaranteed by treaties. A little over a week after Drew's bill reported out of committee, Walter Leeds, Chairman of the Los Angeles delegation in the assembly made a poll of both houses of the legislature and found a majority of the members apparently willing to act in accordance with the wishes of President Roosevelt. "Some of the majority were weak kneed on the [Roosevelt] proposition, and he could not say how they would vote after the matter had been agitated a little more."[39] Governor Gillett remained noncommittal, declaring he would not act until the bills were sent to him. "He and [Senate] Speaker Stanton both are inclined to view the situation as does the president."[40]

Strong public opposition to the Drew bill was expressed by the San Francisco Chamber of Commerce under the leadership of James McNab who sent a written protest against the anti-Japanese legislation. The Chamber of Commerce had been influenced by Francis B. Loomis and sixty businessmen from the commercial organizations of the Pacific Coast who were guests of the Japanese Government in 1908 while the American fleet was in Japan. Loomis believed they all "returned with a fine and just appreciation of the excellent qualities of the Japanese people and with a firm conviction of the good faith and friendly disposition of the Japanese government."[41] On January 22, the Chamber of Commerce of San Francisco forwarded a resolution which stated, in part:

---

[36]Ruth E. McKee, California and her Less Favored Minorities (Washington: War Relocation Authority, 1944), p. 17, cited by F. W. Matson, op. cit., p. 13.

[37]San Francisco Call, January 25, 1909, p. 2/2. Cf. also Hichborn, Legislature of 1909, p. 201.

[38]T. A. Bailey, Theodore Roosevelt and the Japanese-American Crisis, p. 304; Hichborn, Legislature of 1909, p. 203.

[39]San Francisco Call, January 25, 1909, p. 2/1.

[40]San Francisco Call, January 25, 1909, p. 2/2.

[41]San Francisco Call, January 25, 1909, p. 2/1. Matson maintained that the San Francisco Chamber of Commerce established a Japanese American Relations Committee to forestall anti-Japanese legislation and the committee, over a period of years, maintained contact with a similar committee in Japan. F. W. Matson, op. cit., p. 73.

> Whereas, we are of the opinion that the enactment of Assembly bills numers 14, 15, 32, and 78, and Senate bill number 71 will unfavorably affect the growing commerce of the State of California; therefore be it Resolved, that the board of trustees of the Chamber of Commerce of San Francisco respectfully protest against the passage of said bills.[42]

The board of directors of the Los Angeles Chamber of Commerce joined the efforts of the San Francisco branch by writing to the legislature that any action directed at Japanese residents could be taken as an affront by the entire Japanese nation.

> The Oriental trade passing through the ports of this state has assumed large proportions and is likely to be seriously crippled by such proposed action. We therefore respectfully request that action on any of these bills which affect the Japanese people be deferred indefinitely as being unwise and injudicious.[43]

There was growing opposition to discriminating legislation outside California. The board of trade's transportation committee on foreign and insular trade in New York, denounced the "unwisdom of persistent discrimination" against a country such as Japan whose trade is extremely important to the United States. The board of trade was joined by the representatives of General Electric, Kuhn Loeb and Company, A. A. Van Tyn Company and others.[44] The executive council of the Massachusetts state board of trade passed resolutions condemning agitation against Japanese in California.[45] Discriminating legislation against Japanese also appeared in Montana, Oregon, Nebraska and Nevada state legislatures, but all of these measures were killed or tabled in committees.[46]

As the opposition to such legislation began to increase, Governor Gillett presented a special message to the legislature on January 25, 1909. He asked that no laws be passed solely to affect the Japanese people, which would in turn only prove embarrassing to the Federal Government. The legislature should pass only those bills which were absolutely necessary for the state's immediate protection. Gillett insisted that any protest movement would best be handled through channels, and that some statement of facts should be prepared to support any petition to the federal government.

> I would therefore recommend that a sufficient appropriation be made to enable the Labor Commissioner to take a census showing the number of Japanese now in the State, the number classed as laborers, and those classed as agriculturists, the number of acres of land owned by Japanese and the number of acres leased and to get such other and

---

[42] San Francisco Call, January 25, 1909, p. 2/2.

[43] San Francisco Call, January 30, 1909, p. 7/4. The Church Federation Los Angeles joined the Chamber of Commerce in pronunciation against anti-Japanese legislation, San Francisco Call, February 10, 1909, p. 2/1.

[44] San Francisco Call, January 30, 1909, p. 7/4.

[45] San Francisco Call, February 10, 1909, p. 2/1.

[46] San Francisco Call, February 9, 1909, p. 2/3. San Francisco Call, February 10, 1909, p. 2/6; San Francisco Call, February 17, 1909, p. 2/4.

further information as may be useful in making a proper report to
the President of the United States and to Congress. With such a
census we can ascertain hereafter whether or not the Japanese population of this State is increasing or decreasing and whether or
not they are extending their real property holdings.[47]

Governor Gillett also made especial mention of Assembly Bill 78, Drew's alien land law which the governor thought should be made to affect all nations alike instead of discriminating against the citizens of China and Japan. The reaction in the Assembly was a modification of the original bill to one similarly passed in Oklahoma, as the Governor suggested, but Drew fixed the term of leases for two years. The Governor had suggested a longer term.[48] On the following day, the Assembly Judiciary Committee reported favorably on the Drew bill which was made to apply equally to all foreigners and the lease hold was extended to five years.[49] When the bill came up for passage on February 3, Drew found he had only a slight following and was defeated by a vote of 28 to 48.[50] The Call denounced certain members of the legislature as ill advised to propose this

> sort of trivial, nagging legislation .... The measures proposed
> by these people will not in any respect forward the end in view,
> which is exclusion, and quite probably will postpone that desirable conclusion by creating prejudice in the minds of people
> in the ultramontane states. Indeed, the agitation has already
> done California incalculable harm .... Anti-Japanese agitation
> can have only one result at this time. It will so prejudice the
> rest of the country against us that our representatives in
> Washington will not be able to get a hearing when California seeks
> some remedial legislation at the national capital. The trouble
> with the whole matter is that some persons are trying to do cheap
> politics without regard to the gravity of the issues at stake.[51]

The defeat of the Drew bill in the Assembly only frustrated the effects of Senator Sanford, who, along with Burnett of San Francisco and Black of Palo Alto

---

[47] Special Message of Governor James N. Gillett to the Legislature of the State of California, 38th Session, 1909, California Governor's Message, Biennial 1905-1925, pp. 7-8.

[48] San Francisco Call, January 30, 1909, p. 7/4; Hichborn, Legislature of 1909, p. 204.

[49] San Francisco Call, January 31, 1909, p. 36/2.

[50] Hichborn, Legislature of 1909, p. 206. Bailey attributes the defeat of the three important anti-Japanese bills on February 4, to the "vigorous intervention on the part of the federal executive." Bailey, op. cit., p. 308.

[51] San Francisco Call, February 4, 1909, p. 6/1. A half a month later the editor reversed his view: "Although the legislation proposed at Sacramento was ill directed and ineffectual for its prime purpose, it has had the effect to concentrate national attention on Pacific Coast needs in this relation, and to that extent, it has done a useful service. Indeed, the case for exclusion is so strong that it only requires a hearing to be conceded," February 16, 1909, p. 6/1.

on the Committee on Federal Relations denounced Roosevelt and the "big stick" in a joint resolution which passed the Senate with only a few dissenting votes.

> Resolved by the Senate and the Assembly of the State of California jointly that we are unalterably opposed to further Japanese immigration, and urge our representatives in Congress to extend the provisions of the Geary exclusion act so as to include Japanese, Korean, Hindoos and all other Asiatic races; be it further
> Resolved, that we condemn the proposition to naturalize the Japanese and extend the elective franchise to the alien born of that race as being inimical to the welfare of American people.[52]

That same day, Roosevelt had sent a long telegram to speaker Stanton to "go slow" on any action relating to Japanese immigration. Since the joint resolution was only calculated to embarrass the President, Stanton exercised the pocket veto on the resolution even though he broke joint rules in doing so.[53]

The governor's request for a comprehensive investigation of the Japanese was introduced in the legislature on January 28, by Senator Leavitt as Senate Bill 711.[54] The bill was written into the Statutes of California, Chapter 123 and was approved on March 8, 1909. It provided for the compiling of statistics regarding the Japanese in California for the purpose of making a proper report to the President and Congress of those conditions as they actually exist. The governor was given the right to publish and distribute the information gathered. The sum of $10,000 was appropriated to gather the information.[55] The Governor directed John D. Mackenzie, State Labor Commissioner, to begin the investigation of Japanese in California on April 15, 1909. The report was completed on May 20, 1910, and was submitted to the governor on May 23, 1910.[56]

Even before the report was completed, newspapers published information on what would be included in the research and what technique would be used. In May 1909, the Call reported that blanks, four pages in length, were being prepared for every employer of Japanese in the state.

> He will be required to state the number of persons, race, sex, wages with and without board, whether or not they are employed under contract and the reason employed. Pages two and three are

---

[52]San Francisco Call, February 9, 1909, p. 2/4. Senator Burnett had pledged himself to the principles advocated by the Asiatic Exclusion League, A. E. L., Proceedings, March 20, 1910, p. 15.

[53]San Francisco Call, February 9, 1909, p. 1/2; San Francisco Call, March 8, 1909, p. 2/3.

[54]Senate Journal, 1909, p. 323. The bill was withdrawn by Leavitt with unanimous consent on February 23, op. cit., p. 857. The Call later claimed that the work of gathering the information was provided for in Senate bill 711, San Francisco Call, May 13, 1909, p. 4/2.

[55]Statutes of California and Amendments to the Constitution Passed at the Thirty-Eighth Legislature, 1909, Chapter 134, p. 227.

[56]Letter, J. D. Mackenzie, State Labor Commissioner, to Governor Gillett, June 5, 1910, MS, Governor's Papers, RG 7: 106, California State Archives.

devoted exclusively to the conditions of employment, relations between white and Japanese employees, progress of Japanese and the employer's opinion of the relative efficiency of the Japanese and whites. The employer must state how long the Japanese have been in his employ, what race they displaced and the reasons for the change, whether or not their work has been better than that performed by the employees displaced and whether they have aided in the development of new industries.[57]

It would seem that very little of this information was ever published after the original document reached the Governor.[58]

On May 22, 1910, the day before the Mackenzie report was submitted to the Governor, an agreement was reached between the manager of the Association Press at San Francisco and Governor Gillett to permit that news association to review the precise report, "And to make such excerpts as they choose--the work being done wholly in the office, Room 6, Ferry Building, and in the presence of representatives of the Bureau."[59]

Of the newspaper accounts on the Mackenzie report, the Chronicle seems to have given the most space as well as the most objective view of the contents of the report.[60] The investigation covered visits to 4,102 farms in 36 counties. Of this total number of farms, 1,733 were operated by Japanese as owners, cash leasees and share leasees. The remaining 2,369 farms were operated by white farmers who employed a total of 63,198 persons, 53.4 percent of the labor employed was white, 36.4 percent Japanese and 10.2 percent were other races including Chinese, Mexican, Hindus and Indians. On the 1,733 farms operated by Japanese farmers, the total employment of laborers was 17,784, 96 percent were Japanese, while 872 or 4 percent was white laborers producing a crop valued at $28 million dollars.

---

[57]San Francisco Call, May 13, 1909, p. 4/2; San Francisco Call, September 25, 1909, p. 11/2.

[58]The author talked with Dr. W. N. Davis, Chief of Archives, Sacramento, who stated that Governor Gillett took nearly all his records and papers with him when he left office. J. B. Kessler states "An intensive search of archival records, various California libraries, and appropriate State agencies has not produced an original copy of the Mackenzie Report." Kessler, op. cit., p. 26. Daniels claims that "the full report was suppressed; if a copy is still extent no researcher has yet unearthed it from the state archives." R. Daniels, op. cit., p. 131, note 7. Daniels gets most of his ideas from E. G. Mears, op. cit., pp. 444-448. H. A. Millis states that the report was not published. H. A. Millis, The Japanese Problem in the United States, p. 127. A summary of the report may be found in S. L. Gulick, The American-Japanese Problem, Appendix B, pp. 316-23. E. G. Mears, op. cit., Document E gives a brief summary of the Mackenzie Labor Report, pp. 444-448.

[59]Letter, J. D. Mackenzie to Governor Gillett, June 5, 1910. The Fourteenth Biennial Report of Labor Statistics of the State of California, 1909-1910, by Commissioner Mackenzie, devotes only two pages to the Japanese in California; pp. 48-49.

The relationship of crop to percentage of Japanese employed on the 2,369 farms operated by white farmers is as follows: berries, 87.2%; sugar beets, 66.3%; nursery products, 57.3%; grapes, 51.7%; vegetables, 45.7%; citrus fruits, 38.1%; deciduous fruits, 36.5%; miscellaneous, 19.6%; hops, 8.7%; hay and grain, 6.6%.

There was a noticeable difference in the wages paid by white farmers on the basis of race. White laborers were paid $1.38 per day with board and $1.80 per day without board. Japanese were paid $1.49 per day with board and $1.54 per day without board. The average wage paid by Japanese farmers to Japanese laborers was $1.57 per day with board and $1.65 per day without board.

A breakdown of the type of ownership for the 1,733 Japanese farms was: 132 farms were owned; 1,170 farms or 46,480 acres were Japanese cash leasees; and 431 farms or 33,028 acres were Japanese share leasees. The most important crops produced were vegetables worth $2.5 million; deciduous fruit worth $1,750,000; and berries worth $730,000.

The report pointed out the thrift of the Japanese laborer whose "entire existence is regulated on a basis of rigid economy so that he reduced the cost of expenditure for essential subsistence to approximately 20% of his average wage."[61] At all times, the white farmer prefers the white laborer of "good character," but there is not a sufficient number of white laborers to perform the work done by Japanese. The report concludes:

> The competency of both Chinese and Japanese to meet all the requirements in these industries of the orchard, the vineyard and the field, is unquestioned and unquestionable. And the Japanese have proved themselves also capable of the utmost unreliability and arrogant independence. Had the Japanese laborer throttled his ambition to progress along the lines of American citizenship and industrial development, he probably would have attracted small attention of the public mind. Japanese ambition is to progress beyond mere survility to the plane of the better class of America workmen and to own a home with him. The moment that this ambition was exercised, that moment the Japanese ceases to be an ideal laborer.[62]

---

[60] San Francisco Call, May 30, 1910, p. 2/5, is a very brief, factual summary of the report, while Chester H. Rowell of the Fresno Republican entitles the report "A Calamity" and states "It is an official report, and it is going to rise to plague us for a long time to come," cf. E. G. Mears, op. cit., Document E, pp. 446-448.

[61] San Francisco Chronicle, May 30, 1910, p. 15/3-5. There is a typewritten copy of the Chronicle article in the Government Document's Room, Sacramento State Library, under call number I 475-J3.

[62] Ibid. Matson states that "virtually all sections of the agricultural population opposed the upward movement of the Japanese to the status of owners and entrepeneurs .... The small farmer feared direct competition, while the larger agricultural interests resented the loss of their primary labor supply." Matson, op. cit., p. 49.

Such honest and forthright conclusions of prejudice in a state document of some 200,000 words had to be suppressed. The day after the newspapers printed their reviews of the Mackenzie report, the <u>Call</u> interviewed O. A. Tveitmoe who spoke for the Exclusion League and characterized the report as a

> nigger in a wood pile .... The state appropriated $10,000 which we knew at the time was an insufficient amount for a thorough, fair, and comprehensive investigation of the subject .... The railroad companies, other corporations, and large land owners want cheap labor. They would like to transplant some of the dead feudal laws of Europe on American soil, if they only could, in order to exploit the workingmen ... this 200,000 word report to the governor evidently contains more misinformation about the [Japanese] question than any other official document that has so far been produced.[63]

The Exclusion League meeting in June 1910, denounced the report as a document not worthy of serious consideration, by any stretch of the imagination. "McKenzie's [sic] report is his political obituary, at the present writing there is not an aspirant for office in this State who would care to be caught taking a glass of buttermilk with him."[64] An analysis of the report is summed up as "vital, incompetent, immaterial, inadequate, adapted, and prejudicial."[65]

The Building Trades Council, presided over by San Francisco Supervisor John A. Kelly, also an Exclusion League delegate, heard a number of scorching speeches on the alleged laxity of Immigration Commissioners North and Mackenzie. "James G. Maguire thought a better title for the labor commissioner would be, in view of his published [sic] report, 'a special agent of Asiatic help.'"[66]

The editor of the <u>Call</u> joined with labor's dissent of the report. Those who favor the report are stereotyped as that element which are usually found taking the position of cheap and servile labor, and "are not representative" of the majority of Californians.

> The injury that Mackenzie did to California is no doubt real, but we hope not lasting. The argument on our side is so strong and so convincing that it needs only to be presented and it must prevail. This is not primarily an economic question at all, but if it were we should be better off without the Japanese, the Chinese, the Hindus or other Asiatic laborers.[67]

---

[63]San Francisco Call, June 1, 1910, p. 7/2. Tveitmoe was supported by B. B. Rosenthal, Vice President of the San Francisco Labor Council, and Frank Maxwell, Secretary of the Bay Counties District Council of Carpenters, and other labor leaders.

[64]A. E. L., Proceedings, June 19, 1910, p. 26.

[65]Ibid. Pages 26-27.

[66]San Francisco Call, July 6, 1910, p. 2/5.

[67]San Francisco Call, June 28, 1910, p. 4/2.

It was not long, with the dissent of the labor element of the state increasing, until one of the Japanese-baiters in the Senate stepped forward to scuttle the $10,000 report. State Senator Anthony Caminette, a progressive Democrat from Jackson, Amador County, and a "member of the Phelan-Spreckels faction of the Democratic party,"[68] introduced a resolution, seconded by Marc Anthony, on September 9, 1910, that stated:

> The State Labor Commissioner has, in his report concerning Japanese laborers in California, expressed his opinion of the necessity for such laborers in this State, and has thus without authority misrepresented the wishes of the people of this commonwealth; therefore be it
> Resolved, That the opinion of such Labor Commissioner is hereby disapproved by this Senate.[69]

With the "exile" of the labor commissioner's report went the last hope for an objective report on the Japanese in California before the passage of the Alien Land Law of 1913. During the 1911 State Legislature the Democrats, especially Senators Sanford and Caminetti, did all they could to arouse a conflict over the Japanese between Hiram Johnson and President Taft. Early in the session, the Chronicle editor denounced the

> small-bore legislators who seek for personal notoriety by introducing anti-Japanese bills in the legislature and should be summarily squelched .... There is no power to prevent notoriety seekers from introducing pin-pricking anti-Oriental bills at Sacramento, but they should go to committees which will bury them deep. They do not represent public sentiment, because there is no need of them.[70]

The introduction of alien land laws seemed to center in the Senate where four bills were introduced to regulate the ownership of property by aliens: SB2, Larkin;

---

[68] San Francisco Call, September 24, 1912, cited in J. B. Kessler, op. cit., p. 52. It should be remembered that it was Caminetti who appeared before the Exclusion League in 1908 in an attempt to get the League to back the Democratic platform, San Francisco Call, October 19, 1908, p. 7/5. There may have been some party politics involved as Mackenzie was a conservative Republican from San Jose, cf. Daniels, op. cit., p. 131, note 7.

[69] Senate Journal, 1910, p. 39; E. G. Mears, op. cit., p. 444. Mears states that Caminetti was "floor leader of a rather small Democratic minority." In a letter to Nicholas Murray Butler, Irish stated: "Of course we all expected that this [Mackenzie] report, a public document, would be printed for circulation. But the cowardly politicians in the legislature refused to publish it and it exists only in the inaccessible manuscript," Letter, John P. Irish to Nicholas Murray Butler, October, 1913, cited in J. B. Kessler, op. cit., p. 26, note 9.

[70] San Francisco Chronicle, January 19, 1911, p. 6/3. The editor states that "no alien should be permitted to own land in this country," but the law should not be written to discriminate against any nationality or race.

SB 24, Sanford; SB 167, Larkin; and SB 1,074, Finn. None of these Senate bills were reported out of the Assembly.[71]

Not only had the representatives of the Panama-Pacific Exposition taken an active role in killing the bills, but Johnson, Knox and Taft worked together to stop discriminating legislation. On February 23, 1911, Johnson communicated a telegram for President Taft assuring the legislature that Japanese immigration would not be changed in the 1911 treaty with Japan.

> In explanation of this telegram, I convey to you that in December [1910], while in Washington, in conversation with the President, and subsequently with Secretary [of State] Knox, I stated that, in my opinion, the people of the State of California desired Japanese exclusion. The President and the Secretary declared the existing arrangement with Japan [The Gentlemen's Agreement] accomplished this purpose, and that such arrangement would be continued in the future.[72]

Taking a similar position as Senator Sanford and President Roosevelt in the 1909 legislature, Senator Caminetti wired a resolution to President Taft, complaining that the treaty had omitted protective measures vital to the interests of California. The Senator urged the president to withdraw the treaty from further consideration by the Senate of the United States.[73]

Caminetti was not only willing to embarrass the federal government, he was determined to win in his hunt for "Asiatic Angoras," as the Call expressed it. Caminetti had introduced Constitutional Amendment number 29 which would deny suffrage to American-born Asiatics. The Senator saw a grave menace in the increased number of American-born Asiatics[74] who always vote as a unit and may be an agency of harm. Caminetti argued that those people now ineligible for naturalization are a race of "ineligibles" so their children should be denied citizenship.

> We can easily see the time, within but a few years ... when there will be 15,000 or 20,000 Asiatics voting. These people collect in communities and might easily be dominant there. I do not only refer to the Chinese or Japanese but to the Hindus as well, and like peoples.[75]

Such an amendment was to not only arouse the native-born Chinese, but the other "like peoples" who were living in those "communities." They reacted strongly against the amendment as well as Senator Caminetti who arose on a question of personal privilege to withdraw his amendment.

---

[71]Senate Journal, p. 2,364; Hichborn, Legislature of 1911, p. 342.

[72]Journal of the Assembly, 1911, p. 1,187.

[73]San Francisco Call, February 23, 1911, p. 2/2.

[74]George D. Leslie, State Board of Health Commissioner, warned that the Japanese birth rate was increasing--more than double that for 1908. San Francisco Call, March 15, 1909, p. 7/1.

[75]San Francisco Call, February 20, 1911, p. 4/2. Caminetti was opposed by Senator Beban, who introduced many of the prominent native-born Chinese from San Francisco to many of the legislators. Governor Johnson also conferred with the Chinese.

> I never intended to affect any nationality or race ... nor did I intend to prevent the sons of members of such nationality or races from obtaining such privileges. And it was not my purpose to affect any person who is now enjoying such privileges in this State.
>
> The colored citizens of this State have denounced, in unmeasured terms, the proposed amendment, as well as myself. As I never intended, and said amendment did not affect them, or their progeny, I regret their sensitiveness. I have contented myself for this session, to raise the issue and call attention to a coming evil.[76]

As long as there was a Republican Governor and a Republican President, the federal and state authorities were able to keep the Democratic anti-Japanese element in check. That none of the discriminating bills were sent to the Governor testifies to this generalization. The 1912 election was to change this federal-state balance on the Japanese issue. As Senator Sanford stated in December 1911: "The people of the Pacific Coast have become weary and disgusted with the unpatriotic and un-American manner in which those in high authority at Washington have been handling the immigration question."[77] The election of 1912 was to be truly unique in American history.

---

[76] Senate Journal, 1911, p. 2,673.

[77] San Francisco Call, December 6, 1911, p. 8/2. Sanford was on the Executive Committee of the 1908 Democratic Campaign with James Phelan, San Francisco Call, September 13, 1908, p. 20/3. His anti-Oriental bill, SB 24, was introduced on January 5, 1911, and was quoted in Knox to Johnson, January 19, 1911, State Department. Papers, 811.52/2; also in Johnson Papers, cited in Kessler, op. cit., p. 16.

In a letter to Phelan after the 1911 Legislature, Sanford complained: "the manner in which the bill was defeated in the Assembly was most cowardly .... I am going after this alien land bill in a red hot way. I shall be pleased to receive any suggestion from you that you may see fit to give." Letter, Sanford to Phelan, April 6, 1911 (Phelan MSS), cited in Daniels, op. cit., p. 54; 133.

CHAPTER VI

THE ALIEN LAND LAW OF 1913: GRAPE JUICE DIPLOMACY
AND A BIT OF POLITICAL BUNCOMBE

"when the State chooses a lawless course, the task of altering that course is great The State has limitless resources, its victims relatively few And the State is often cruelly impersonal, separate and is greater than the sum of its human parts."

>William Hogan, "Patriotism and Dynamite," San Francisco Sunday Examiner and Chronicle, "This World," April 23, 1967, p. 34.

"It [the passage of the alien land law] is just a bit of cheap political buncombe, meaningless and ineffective in itself, useful only in that it may help somebody to get votes under pretense of being a Japanese baiter."

>San Francisco Argonaut, April 12, 1913, cited in San Francisco Call, April 30, 1913, p. 10/7.

CHAPTER VI

THE ALIEN LAND LAW OF 1913: GRAPE JUICE DIPLOMACY
AND A BIT OF POLITICAL BUNCOMBE

Passage of the Alien Land Law of 1913 was the direct result of the election of 1912, for it was the first time since the Japanese school incident of 1906 that there was a progressive Democratic President in office while there was a progressive Republican governor in office in California. It is interesting to note that during the 1910 state election, all three California parties contained anti-Oriental declarations.[1] The Democratic platform contained two anti-Oriental planks: number seven, demanded the exclusion of all Asiatic labor and plank number twenty advocated "the adoption of the Sanford bill, preventing Asiatics who are not eligible to citizenship in America from owning land in California."[2] The Republican platform, plank sixteen stated: "We declare our faith in the unswerving opposition of the people of California to the further admission of Oriental laborers, and we urge on Congress and the President the adoption of all necessary measures to guard against this evil."[3]

The presidential campaign of 1912 brought increased agitation in the State Democratic party, while the Republican State and national platforms were silent on the anti-Oriental issue.[4] The Democratic national platform was written by Wilson, Bryan and Senator O'Gorman and "they absolutely omitted an immigration plank, though

---

[1] F. W. Matson, The Anti-Japanese Movement in California, 1890-1942, p. 23.

[2] Sacramento Bee, September 7, 1910, p. 13/3; Hichborn, Legislature of 1911, pp. xxv-xxvi. Sanford's campaign circular during the 1910 election complained of intervention by the "big stick" and that "no race of people that cannot become citizens of the United States should be allowed to gain a foothold in this country," Hichborn, Legislature of 1913, pp. 223-224. Sanford's phraseology was used by the Asiatic Exclusion League in an almost exact restatement: A. E. L., Proceedings, November 17, 1912, p. 267.

[3] San Francisco Call, September 7, 1910, p. 2/3; Sacramento Bee, September 7, 1910, p. 12/7; Hichborn, Legislature of 1911, p. xxiv.

[4] J. B. Kessler, The Political Factors in California Anti Alien Land Legislation, 1912-1913, p. 51. The Sacramento Union, September 24, 1912, says that Chester H. Rowell practically wrote the Republican platform, cf. also the San Francisco Call, November 26, 1912, p. 18/1.

The Asiatic Exclusion League passed a resolution urging Governor Johnson and Theodore Bell to obtain in the Republican and Democratic platforms a plank pledging exclusion of all Asiatic laborers. San Francisco Call, June 17, 1912, p. 12/7.

they received an avalanche of telegrams and pleas."[5] The California Democratic party leadership changed in 1912 from control by Theodore Bell to the Phelan-McNab forces. The Call noted that both Bell and Phelan were anti-Oriental and that the Southern California Democrats did not clamor for Phelan as state central committee chairman.[6]

Since the California Democrats did not obtain an anti-Oriental plank in the national platform, Phelan saw to it that Wilson published such a statement on May 3, 1912.[7] California Democrats used Wilson's statement as propaganda by distribution of a card representing Wilson as the champion of Asiatic exclusion and Theodore Roosevelt as an advocate of Japanese naturalization.[8] The card was circulated after the attempted assassination of Theodore Roosevelt and while Hiram Johnson stayed in the East to meet Roosevelt's speaking schedule. Perhaps one of the strongest reasons for obtaining the anti-Oriental statement from Wilson was to bring the national Democratic platform into conformity and consistency with the California State Democratic Platform which stated:

> 30. We demand immediate federal legislation for the exclusion of Japanese, Korean and Hindoo laborers, and impose on our candidates for the Senate and Assembly the duty of working for that end by legislation, resolutions and all other honorable means open to them as state legislators.
> 31. We favor the passage of a bill that will prevent any alien not eligible to citizenship from owning land in the state of California.[9]

It was these planks which caused an ever widening political gulf between Democrats and Progressive Republicans, and it seems that Senator Sanford, with the assistance of James Phelan, insisted on these discriminating planks to create a political issue and keep their names in the papers. Along with Senator Caminetti, both Phelan and Sanford had political motives behind their desires to save California

---

[5]J. B. Kessler, op. cit., p. 48; A. E. L., Proceedings, July 1912, p. 235.

[6]San Francisco Call, September 21, 1912, p. 11/1; San Francisco Call, September 29, 1912, p. 9/3. As a result, J. O. Davis was elected Chairman of the State Central Committee and Davis declared that "while Phelan has done nothing by way of a campaign for cabinet recognition, the San Francisco man stands well with Wilson personally and is being considered for a portfolio," San Francisco Call, December 24, 1912, p. 20/1.

[7]Cf. Robert E. Hennings, "James D. Phelan and the Woodrow Wilson Anti-Oriental Statement of May 3, 1912," California Historical Society Quarterly, 42 (December 1963), pp. 291-300.

[8]Letter, J. O. Davis to Joseph P. Tumulty, January 4, 1913, State Department Papers, 811.52/34. Cited in J. B. Kessler, op. cit., p. 55, note 54.

[9]Sacramento Union, in Hugh Bradford's Scrapbook (n.p.), California Room, Sacramento State Library; Hichborn, Legislature of 1913, p. 213. The Sanford Bill--SB 24, provided that "no alien who is not [sic] eligible to citizenship" shall hold real property in California, cf. Hichborn, Legislature of 1911, p. 342.

for the white man. Before the end of 1913, Anthony Caminetti, the first Italian-American to be elected to Congress, was appointed as Commissioner of Immigration,[10] and James Phelan announced his candidacy for the Senatorship from California.[11] The one unsuccessful candidate of the anti-Oriental triumvirate was John Banyon Sanford who announced his candidacy for governor on the Democratic ticket in January 1914.[12]

Shortly before the 1913 legislative session, Sanford let it be known to Republicans at a banquet celebrating Wilson's victory in 1912, that he intended to continue his anti-Japanese campaign. In a long letter to Theodore Roosevelt, Hiram Johnson reported that:

> at the banquet, Sanford announced to those near him, that on the first day of the session, he was going to introduce an alien land bill, and that he would have that fellow Johnson side stepping and climbing over the capitol dome during all the rest of the session with that bill. The democrat sitting next to him said, 'Be careful, Senator, remember there will be then a democratic national administration, and you may have that administration side stepping.' Sanford's boasting replay was 'Don't trouble about that. Mr. Bryan and Mr. Wilson know all about this question and we will have Johnson jumping during this whole session.' Mr. Bryan didn't laugh as heartily at this narrative as my friend had thought he would. I might remark, parenthetically, Sanford is still side stepping. He was one of the democrats [who] is a candidate for a job.[13]

---

[10] John Higham, Strangers in the Land, Patterns of American Nativism, 1860-1925, p. 228. Higham believed that Wilson had taken the control of the bureau out of the hands of labor leaders as an earnest desire to placate the European immigrants. The Call stated that "Mr. Caminetti, the father, has recently been appointed commissioner general of immigration because of his prominence in democratic politics and not for any known efficiency. Mr. Caminetti, the son, is under indictment for violation of the Mann Act," San Francisco Call, June 24, 1913, p. 2/3. Just a few days after his appointment, Caminetti was present in Washington when Phelan gave a banquet for W. J. Bryan. Some of the most prominent California anti-Oriental agitators were in attendance: Congressmen Kahn and Raker, Franklin K. Lane, Carlos McClatchy, and Ira S. Bennett, a Call correspondent, San Francisco Call, June 27, 1913, p. 4/3. There is some evidence that Caminetti made a profit from the passage of an alien land law. He and his descendants now own land in the Japanese section of Walnut Grove and are making increased profits by raising the rent on the land. Cf. Sacramento Bee, January 14, 1968, p. A8/3-5.

[11] In June 1913, Phelan met Wilson in Washington and declined "appointment as Ambassador to Austria, offered to him several weeks ago by Secretary Bryan. Mr. Phelan intends to run for the United States Senate in California next year." San Francisco Call, June 24, 1913, p. 1/2.

[12] Cf. San Francisco Examiner, January 22, 1914, p. 2/5.

[13] Letter, H. W. Johnson to Theodore Roosevelt, June 21, 1913, cited in Daniels, op. cit., pp. 116-117. It was the Sanford Bill, SB 27, that the Asiatic Exclusion League insisted on--even if its passage meant war. A. E. L., Proceedings, February 1913, p. 293-94. Cf. also San Francisco Call, January 20, 1913, p. 14/5.

In all, there were some thirty-four anti-Japanese bills introduced by both parties in the California Legislature between March and May 1913,[14] and it has been maintained that "California's organized farmer and labor groups solidly approved of the alien land bills under consideration."[15]

However, an intensive examination of Hiram Johnson's letters indicate little demand for discriminating legislation from the farm areas. As Kessler has stated,

> The Governor's correspondence files, which are remarkably complete, contain no communications on anti-alien legislation until March 17, 1913 .... Not until the latter part of April, when the issue was given a great deal of publicity in the press was there a marked increase in the Governor's public mail on this subject. On May 15, 1913, the greatest volume of mail was addressed to the Governor--a total of 47 letters. On only seven other days during the entire controversy was there a similar volume of mail dealing with anti-alien legislation.[16]

It was not until April 22, 1913, that the Call reported there were hundreds of messages pouring into Sacramento from all over the San Joaquin Valley against the Japanese.[17]

Since public interest was not widely aroused until after the middle of March 1913, it would seem that the main cause of the passage of the Alien Land Law in 1913 rests upon the clash between federal and state authorities and most especially upon the unique character of California's "Prodigal Son," Hiram W. Johnson. He had already been caught off guard in the Presidential election and he was not about to make any hasty decisions which would give the Democrats a political issue in the state's 1914 election.[18]

---

[14] P. E. Coletta, "The Most Thankless Task," p. 170.

[15] Ibid. Coletta may have obtained this idea from Franklin Hichborn who stated: "The effective support of the policy of the bills came from the farming district where Asiatics had gained a foothold," Legislature of 1913, p. 225. As Daniels has pointed out, much of Hichborn's work was subsidized by Rudolph Spreckels and James D. Phelan. As both a "reformer and prohibitionist," Hichborn's view of the Japanese does not always tell the whole story, Daniels, op. cit., p. 131, note 7.

[16] J. B. Kessler, op. cit., p. 70, note 2. Kessler also examined the Los Angeles Examiner, San Diego Union, San Francisco Chronicle, San Francisco Call, Sacramento Union and Sacramento Bee for the month of December and failed to disclose a widespread popular demand for anti-Oriental legislation, Ibid.

[17] Ibid., p. 7, note 25.

[18] Robert Hennings states that "it was not until several months after the [1912] election that Johnson discovered just what had one on" and his "chief complaints about the California campaign centered on personal grounds." Op. cit., 295-96; 299, note 32.

Johnson was not only suspicious of Democratic motives, but he was given every reason to believe that the Democrats were "playing politics" with the Alien Land Law issue.[19] James B. Kessler, in an examination of the Johnson-Rowell papers, revealed those incidents which caused the Governor to suspect his political enemies of seeking to exploit his willingness to cooperate with the Federal Government.[20] In response to a letter from Johnson, Rowell warned the Governor:

> His policy [Wilson's] and your policy apparently coincide exactly, but he seems to be determined that you shall take the whole responsibility for it, and that his irresponsible partisans in California shall have full liberty to make all the demogogic capital against you they can by advocating a policy of which he himself disapproves and desires to prevent, but which he wishes you to take the whole responsibility of preventing. It is a petty and cowardly attitude upon the part of the President, and I hope it will be possible to smoke him out into saying absolutely and officially the things which he so freely said to you privately and confidentially.[21]

Wilson's apparent refusal to personally appeal to Johnson was further substantiated by the fact that all of the President's contacts with the Governor before April 22, were made <u>through</u> known anti-Oriental legislators.

> On March 17, Johnson wrote to Rowell, the situation [relating to the proposed alien land bills] is unique and interesting now, and not only interesting, but one of which we can get a good deal of satisfaction. [Democratic State Senator Anthony] Caminetti apparently comes authoritatively to ask that we go slow with Japanese legislation. This is confidential. I think before the session adjourns the present administration at

---

[19]Ironically, Wilson thought Governor Johnson was "playing politics" and stated it publicly. Cf. P. E. Coletta, op. cit., p. 169. On April 24, the Call editorial stated: "It is to be confessed that there are signs of playing politics at Sacramento. If this is the case, it is time to stop playing politics, Washington evidently is trying to play politics. Washington should be warned. Don't play politics with dynamite!" San Francisco Call, April 24, 1913, p. 6/2.

[20]J. B. Kessler, op. cit., p. xi. Kessler concludes that "whatever influence groups may have exercised in the shaping of the content of the legislation, its enactment cannot be explained merely as the result of group pressures. The Governor's personality as it was influenced by his perception of the issue was the decisive factor." Ibid., p. 186.

[21]Letter, Rowell to Johnson, April 9, 1913, Rowell Papers, cited in Kessler, op. cit., p. 131. The Democrats in the legislature were well aware of the fact that Wilson had not communicated with Johnson. Senator Caminetti stated: "I don't anticipate any request from Washington asking this legislation to recede. It is proper for Washington to ask for information at all times." Sacramento Bee, April 5, 1913, p. 5/5-6.

Washington may be asking us in exactly the same fashion as previous administrations have asked us, to take no position.[22]

Wilson's choice of an intermediary, William Kent, seems to have been a poor one.[23] On the very day he was chosen by the President to act as an intermediary, Kent informed Bryan that he approved "the proposed legislation in California directed against ownership of land by aliens ineligible for citizenship."[24] Kent himself helped to heighten Governor Johnson's suspicions of the President's motives.

> The result of our conference [between Kent and Wilson] was, that it should be suggested that a bill might be drawn excluding from land ownership those who had not made application for American citizenship, thereby leaving the way open for bonafide prospective citizens to participate in the privilege of owning California land, but excluding those who had no such intent, necessarily including the Japanese whose first papers would not be accepted. The situation was a most delicate one. I wired Governor Johnson the suggestion, not stating its source--this on the Western Union--and then on the Postal line, I sent another wire, stating that the suggestion was from the highest possible source. Johnson wired back that the President must show his hand, and I thereafter naturally refrained from any further communication. In this episode there was the clearest of evidence that Johnson was supremely anxious to put President Wilson in the hole, and his telegram practically insinuated as much.[25]

Theodore Roosevelt later confided to Johnson that Kent and Wilson were playing politics.

> Billy Kent played the part of a stool pigeon for Wilson. I think he is entirely sincere and well-meaning, but ... any

---

[22]Letter, Johnson to Rowell, March 17, 1915, Rowell MSS, cited in Daniels, op. cit., p. 59; 135. Wilson appealed to Gompers and the California State Federation of Labor to withhold its demands for an anti-Japanese land law. Gompers reports, "I told him [Wilson] I would do the best I could and drafted a telegram to Paul Scharrenberg which I showed to him. Mr. Tumulty took the telegram in to show the President and returned with the statement that in his opinion it would be materially helpful." Gomper, op. cit., p. 60-61. These actions naturally made the Progressives even more suspicious of Wilson's motives.

[23]Kent's wife later wrote: "The man whom President Wilson subsequently selected to act as intermediary in an effort to prevent legislation offensive to Japan was an ardent supporter of Asiatic exclusion." Elizabeth Kent, William Kent, Independent (Kentfield: By the author, 1950), pp. 209-210, cited in Kessler, op. cit., p. 57.

[24]Letter, Kent to Bryan, April 7, 1913, Kent Papers, cited in Kessler, op. cit., p. 120.

[25]Kent MSS, cited in Kessler, op. cit., p. 123; cf. also Johnson to Rowell, April 8, 1913, Rowell Papers.

man who can support Wilson and try to play Wilson's game against
you as in this instance, and who yet voted for me last year, and
capped the climax by voting for Mann [Republican leader in the
House of Representatives] for Speaker, threads such a maze of
devious intricacies, and has a mind which must be filled with
such a queer jumble of contradictions, that, however much one
may like him personally, there is very little good to be gotten
out of him from the public standpoint.[26]

For many weeks Johnson waited for a direct communication from the President. When it did materialize, Wilson was not only sarcastic, but he made it seem that Johnson, and not the vacillations of the President, was responsible for the circumstances which promoted the delay. The President's telegram was sent in response to a message from Johnson stating that California desired to co-operate with the Federal Government to avoid international troubles. Wilson retorted:

Thank you for your patriotic telegram. We find it so difficult
from this distance to understand fully the situation with regard
to the sentiments and circumstances lying back of the pending
proposition concerning the ownership of land in your state that I
venture to inquire whether it would be agreeable to you and the
Legislature to have the Secretary of State visit Sacramento for
the purpose of counseling with you and the members of the Legislature and co-operating with you and them in the framing of a
law which would meet the views of the People of the State and
yet leave untouched the international obligation of the United
States.[27]

William J. Bryan viewed the object of his trip to California in April 1913, as an impossible task. He told Josephus Daniels, "Wish me well, my friend, in what promises to be the most thankless task I ever undertook."[28] The California Progressives were just as skeptical as the Secretary of State. They all anxiously awaited the President's trump card. Johnson later confided to Roosevelt:

---

[26]Theodore Roosevelt to Johnson, June 20, 1913. Johnson Papers, cited in Kessler, op. cit., p. 123, note 73. Kent later cabled Johnson: "Congratulations upon your brave stand, opinion universally with you here. Any demands by foreign nations that we should regulate our international affairs to suit them is hostile impudence. The treaty making power is not supreme in such questions as ours." Sacramento Bee, April 27, 1913, p. 18/4. It would seem that Johnson later evened the score with Kent in the 1920 election by supporting Samuel M. Shortridge over the "distinguished progressive," William Kent. Cf. Bean, op. cit., p. 363.

[27]Sacramento Bee, April 23, 1913, p. 1/1; cf. P. E. Coletta, op. cit., p. 169. The New York World later reported that Johnson's response to the President's telegram was: "To hell with Wilson. Let's put him in a hole." Johnson denied this story claiming that it was manufactured by a reporter on the staff of the Sacramento Union. Letter, Johnson to V. S. McClatchy, May 8, 1913, Johnson Papers, cited in Kessler, op. cit., p. 179.

[28]P. E. Coletta, op. cit., p. 170.

> We all thought, of course, that he was coming here with something
> of great importance to import, and the gravity of the situation
> was during this period of waiting, more keenly felt than at any
> other time .... After sitting all day, Mr. Bryan presented abso-
> lutely nothing that could not have been transmitted within the
> limits of a night letter, without using all of the allotted words,
> and at the conclusion of the first consultation, there was a
> feeling among the legislators not only of disappointment, but
> that they had been decoyed more or less into a postponement without
> any real reasons, and that their time in consultation and confer-
> ence had simply been frittered away.[29]

What Johnson and the legislators did not know at the time was that Bryan had come to California with more than a desire to confer. His intent seems to have been one of "friendly persuasion." Franklin Hichborn, in an interview with J. B. Kessler, reported that

> Bryan thought that the legislature, in enacting an anti-alien
> land law, would be committed by the State Constitution [of 1879]
> to pass a bill discriminating against Asiatics .... Hichborn
> was not convinced and discovered subsequently that the section
> to which Bryan referred was repealed by constitutional amendment
> in 1894.[30]

Bryan intended to cite Article 1, Section 17, of the State Constitution which originally read

> "Foreigners of white races or of African descent, eligible to
> become citizens of the United States under the naturalization
> laws thereof, while bona fide residents of this State, shall
> have the rights in respect to the acquisition, possession,
> enjoyment, transmission, and inheritance of all property [other
> than real estate] as native born citizens ..."[31]

He seems to have been unaware of the fact that in 1894, the Constitution was amended by the addition of the four bracketed words which invalidated the Secretary's constitutional argument.

However, the Progressives were determined to draw Bryan out into the open. Even before the Secretary of State had arrived in Sacramento, a tour of Florin had been arranged.[32] On April 30, Bryan, Johnson, and Assemblyman Hugh Bradford traveled through Florin and Walnut Grove in the Governor's car. Johnson commented that he

---

[29]Letter, Johnson to Roosevelt, June 21, 1913, cited in Daniels, op. cit., p. 114. Cf. also, E. R. Penrose, "Grape Juice Diplomacy and a Bit of Political Buncombe," Pacific Historical Review, XXXVII (May 1968), 161.

[30]J. B. Kessler, op. cit., pp. 181-82; San Francisco Examiner, April 25, 1917, p. 4/1.

[31]West's Annotated California Codes, p. 526-27. Cf. Penrose, op. cit., p. 161.

[32]Hugh Bradford, Scrapbook, Sacramento State Library (n.p.), contains a list of legislators who contributed to the car pool.

was pleased that Bryan had accepted the invitation to see for himself "California's best argument for an anti-alien land law."³³ Bradford conducted the Governor and the Secretary of State through the Florin area, pointing out the school rooms in which "it was noted that little white children were 'sandwiched' in between little brown boys and girls."³⁴ Bryan's comments to all this propaganda was couched in the best diplomatic phrases: "It was a very pleasant ride. I have seen not only a Japanese settlement, but also a beautiful valley."³⁵

Bryan's mission in California proved to be not only a "thankless task," but even probably strengthened the legislator's determination to resist federal intervention "at the hands of state-rights Democrats like Bryan and Wilson."³⁶

While the most important reasons for the passage of the Webb-Honey Bill on May 19 seemed to be state-federal conflicts, party politics, and personality issues, some of the responsibility must also rest on those newspapers and individuals who encouraged discriminating legislation against California's Japanese population.

Between March 19 and April 2, the California Senate Judiciary Committee and the Joint Senate and Assembly Judiciary Committees met for the purpose of listening to public opinion on the need for anti-alien legislation. Hichborn reports that men stood with tears streaming down their faces while stating that white farmers were holding

> a deadline at Elk Grove now, beyond which the brown man cannot pass. If we are denied relief from the situation that confronts us, I will not be responsible for what will surely happen.³⁷

Others who addressed the Judiciary Committee on March 19 were representatives of labor organizations, the Asiatic Exclusion League, and farmers from Elk Grove and Florin.³⁸ The Joint Senate and Assembly Judiciary Committee met on April 2 to listen to "representative Californians--farmers, laborers and capitalists."³⁹ One of the so-called "farmers," Ralph Newman,⁴⁰ emotionally appealed to the crowd packed in the Senate Chamber.

---

³³*San Francisco Call*, May 1, 1913, p. 2/4.

³⁴*Sacramento Bee*, May 1, 1913, p. 1/1.

³⁵*Ibid.*

³⁶P. E. Coletta, *op. cit.*, p. 171.

³⁷Hichborn, *Legislature of 1913*, p. 225. This farmer, M. A. Mitchell, was present along with Ralph Newman, Paul Scharrenberg, James D. Phelan and Grove Johnson at the April 2 committee meeting, cf. *Sacramento Bee*, April 3, 1913, p. 4/4-5.

³⁸*San Francisco Call*, March 19, 1913, cited in Kessler, *op. cit.*, p. 103.

³⁹*Sacramento Bee*, April 3, 1913, p. 1/3. The article was written by Hichborn.

⁴⁰Daniels states that Newman was an ex-Congregational minister. Daniels, *op. cit.*, p. 59; 135, note 69.

> Near my home is an eighty-acre tract of as fine land as there is
> in California. On that land lives a Japanese. With that
> Japanese lives a white woman. In that woman's arms is a baby.
> What is that baby? It isn't a Japanese. It isn't white. I'll
> tell you what that baby is. It is a germ of the mightiest prob-
> lem that ever faced this State; a problem that will make the
> black problem of the South look white.
> All about us the Asiatics are gaining a foothold. They are
> setting up Asiatic standards. From whole communities, the white
> are moving out. Already the blood is intermingling. At present
> the problem is comparatively easy and can be snuffed out.[41]

Like speeches were given by R. C. Hearst, Paul Scharrenberg and James D. Phelan so that those who were prepared to present information favorable to the Japanese were not heard. Alice M. Brown and her colleagues from Florin complained to David S. Jordan:

> We were denied an opportunity to be heard. Instead, three of
> the so-called, ignorant and rancorous, were called upon by the
> chair, and given the floor in preference to us.[42]

Some newspapers were also guilty of restricting information in favor of the Japanese. The Call, for instance, gave Sanford's propaganda front page status:

> People demanding enactment of alien land law. If legislature re-
> fuses, people will resort to initiative sentiment. Five to one
> in favor of alien land law. Government should not interfere with
> our local affairs. Hands off at Washington. Japs own 52,000
> acres of land, lease 400,000 acres. More information to come.[43]

Thirteen days later, the Call printed George Shima's response to Sanford--on page two:

> At present the Japanese own only 20,000 acres of land in California
> and not 50,000 acres as has been reported and they lease only 170,000

---

[41]Hichborn, Legislature of 1913, pp. 230-31; Elk Grove Citizen, April 10, 1913, p. 1/1; Sacramento Bee, April 3, 1913, p. 4/4-5.

[42]Letter, Alice M. Brown to D. S. Jordan, April 6, 1913, cited in Kessler, op. cit., p. 107. She wrote articles which the press refused to print. Cf. San Francisco Chronicle, January 16, 1915, p. 77/1-7 as an example of Miss Brown's concern for a more objective view of Japanese in the Florin area.

[43]San Francisco Call, April 10, 1913, p. 1/1; Kessler, op. cit., p. 128; Bailey, op. cit., p. 52. These figures are further circulated as truth; cf. Layman Abbott, "The Alien Land Bill in California," The Outlook, 104 (April 19, 1913), 828.

acres and not 400,000 acres as reported. I believe, personally, that Oriental labor will be almost necessary in certain rural districts of California.[44]

Far too often, information in favor of the Japanese was either ignored by the press, or the information appeared under "advertisement" which meant that Japanese, and those who wanted to express their views in favor of Orientals had to pay for the space.[45]

The signing of the Webb-Honey Bill into law on May 19, 1913, was to satisfy few who desired it. The Asiatic Exclusion League, still functioning in May, was strongly opposed to the law with lease privileges.[46] The law seems to have been equally unsatisfactory for some farmers since it

> did nothing more than prevent the acquisition of real property by the Japanese in the future. It did not deprive them of land which they already owned. It did not even prevent them from leasing any amount of land they might wish in the future. Although the leasing term was limited to three years, they might legally renew the lease and remain on the land indefinitely. The law, therefore was absolutely inefficient in removing the Japanese from the land.[47]

The Alien Land Law did not satisfy some legislators--especially those who wanted to repeal the three year lease privileges. William R. Shartel, an attorney from Modoc County in the Republican Party, and owner of the Martinez Daily Standard, introduced Assembly Bill 612 on January 22, 1915, to "repeal certain provisions in relation to the right to lease lands for agricultural purposes."[48] He believed that the time has passed for the need of leasing rights in the 1913 law and he "intended

---

[44] San Francisco Call, April 23, 1913, p. 2/3. Strangely enough, the Senator who was most effective in voiding the 1909 Japanese census, Anthony Caminetti, sponsored another bill, SB 1783 on May 9, 1913, to provide for a census of the Japanese population in California, cf. San Francisco Call, May 10, 1913, p. 2/2; Senate Journal, p. 2757. This bill was left in the Finance Committee. Senate Final History, Fortieth Session, p. 26.

[45] San Francisco Call, April 30, 1913, p. 10/1-7; May 4, 1913, p. 26/6; May 4, 1913, p. 24/1-7; May 7, 1913, p. 5/1-7.

[46] The three year lease amendment was proposed by Senator Boynton who believed that "many Japanese laborers would remain in the state and not bring a shortage in the labor supply." San Francisco Call, May 3, 1913, p. 1/1; 10/1-2. The Alien Land Law, as passed by the 1913 Legislature, is in Appendix C.

[47] R. L. Buell, "The Development of Anti-Japanese agitation in the United States, II," p. 65. Cf. also San Francisco Call, May 10, 1913, p. 1/7; San Francisco Call, July 29, 1913, p. 2/5; W. V. Woehlke, "White and Yellow in California," The Outlook, 104 (May 10, 1913), 61-65.

[48] Franklin Hichborn, Legislature of 1916, p. 230; F. W. Matson, op. cit., p. 13; John A. Gothberg, The Japanese in California and the 1920 Fight for Land Rights, pp. 13-15.

to continue his efforts to have the bill passed notwithstanding Governor Johnson's statement that he would veto the bill if it should reach him."[49] Johnson stood unalterably opposed to any further discriminating legislation in 1915.[50]

The Alien Land Law was changed by an initiative measure, Proposition One, on the November 1920, ballot, and subsequently by the State Legislature in 1923 due to court action voiding certain sections of the law.[51] However, the final repeal of the Alien Land Law did not occur until after the opposition of the Japanese Exclusion League, formed in 1919-1920, had lost its public appeal in California. Sentiment against Japanese ownership of land seems to have changed by 1944 when Assistant Attorney General, James H. Oakley, proposed an initiative measure be drawn up to extend the Land Law of 1920 to include all "persons of Japanese ancentry."[52] The measure was intended to make it economically impossible for persons of Japanese descent to earn a living in California after World War II. E. A. Murry, a Los Angeles public relations consultant, who directed the campaign for the Japanese Exclusion Association, stated that, "Some organizations make a lot of noise about the Japanese and are interested until they are asked to give a little money .... I had to finance most of the campaign myself."[53] To qualify for the November ballot, the petition required 178,764 signatures. The petition filed bore only 77,875 signatures.[54]

Another attempt to reinforce the Land Law of 1920, appeared on the November 1946, ballot as Proposition 15. The measure was intended to tighten the 1920 and 1923 legislative amendments to the law of 1913.[55] The Bee recommended passage of the proposition and commented in an editorial that

> The California State Supreme Court issued an important decision on Thursday [November 1, 1946], reaffirming provisions of the Alien Land Act prohibiting aliens ineligible to citizenship from owning agricultural land in this state .... This proposition is designed to validate amendments to the Alien Land Act to prevent subterfuges such as the one present in the Supreme Court case. Its' passage would simply tighten the law to prevent trickery and circumvention of the 1913 law by aliens already barred from agricultural land ownership in this state. That is all. Vote yes on No. 15.[56]

---

[49]San Francisco Examiner, January 26, 1915, p. 6/1.

[50]Gothberg, op. cit., p. 15; Matson, op. cit., p. 109; cf. Final Calendar of Legislative Business, 1915, p. 668.

[51]California Statutes, 1923, p. 1020. Cf. I. B. Cross, op. cit., p. 340. The Alien Land Laws of 1920 and 1923 are in Appendices D and E.

[52]San Francisco Chronicle, March 12, 1944, p. 10/3.

[53]San Francisco Chronicle, September 11, 1944, p. 7/4. A new organization, the Japanese Exclusion Association, was formed under Articles of Incorporation on February 14, 1944, cf. Secretary of State, Inactive Corporation File, #194,195, California State Archives, Sacramento, California.

[54]Ibid.

[55]California, Secretary of State, Statement of Vote at General Election held on November 5, 1946, p. 37.

[56]Sacramento Bee, November 2, 1946, p. 26; San Francisco Chronicle, November 2, 1946, p. 8, recommended a no vote.

The proposition was defeated by a vote of 1,143,780 to 797,067, indicating that opposition to the Japanese ownership of land was no longer effective.[57]

The Land Laws of 1913, 1920, and 1923 remained in effect until 1952, when the State Supreme Court in a four-to-three decision ruled that the laws violated the due process and equal protection clauses of the Fourteenth Amendment. The Chronicle commented:

> The State Supreme Court ruling was made on the case of Sei Fujii, a Los Angeles newspaper publisher who bought property there in 1948 as a test case. The State Attorney General's office held that the land escheated to the State ... because Fujii's ownership was illegal.[58]

Chief Justice Phillip Gibson, in a majority opinion, stated that the Alien Land Law was

> obviously designed and administered as an instrument for effectuating racial discrimination .... It does not follow that a person has no stake in the economy and social fortune of a State merely because the Federal law denies him the right to naturalization. His American-born children are citizens, and having made his home here, he has a natural interest identical with that of an eligible alien .... The real purpose of the law ... was the elimination of competition by alien Japanese in farming California land, and this discriminating nature renders it invalid under the constitution.[59]

The decision of the State Supreme Court ended the escheatment of land by the state, but the land law remained on the statute books until November 1956, because the 1920 law stated if any part of the law was declared unconstitutional, the remainder of the bill was not invalidated. It was this remaining part of the land law which was placed on the 1956 ballot as Proposition 13. There was no opposition to the repeal of the Alien Land Law which was finally made inoperative by a vote of 2,801,951 to 1,391,991. Every county had passed a majority of 'yes' votes to repeal the law.[60]

It had taken the people of California more than forty years to repeal a discriminating law created by yellow journalism, labor unions, party politics, cheap politicians, and job seekers such as John Sanford, James D. Phelan, Walter MacArthur, Anthony Caminetti, Paul Scharrenberg,[61] Hugh Bradford, J. M. Inman and many others.

---

[57] Statement of the vote, p. 37.

[58] San Francisco Chronicle, April 18, 1952, p. 2/1.

[59] Ibid.

[60] California, Secretary of State, Statement of the Vote at General Election held on November 6, 1956, p. 18.

[61] Hiram Johnson appointed Scharrenberg a member of the State Immigration Commission shortly after the Alien Land Law was passed. Cf. San Francisco Examiner, September 18, 1913, p. 2/8; J. B. Kessler, op. cit., p. 76; I. B. Cross, op. cit., p. 330; Bean, op. cit., p. 331.

With all of these groups and individuals working for the common goals of discrimination and exclusion, public opinion was molded into an organized opposition to the Japanese in California. As Kee Owyang, Panama-Pacific Exposition Commissioner from China and former Consul General at San Francisco, once so aptly observed:

> It seems much easier to enter Heaven than to set foot on the American Continent. All this agitation has been directed against the Chinese [and Japanese] by political demagogues who have resorted to misrepresentation, falsehood, and vehemence to secure their political jobs and favors.[62]

---

[62]San Francisco Examiner, August 11, 1915, p. 6/2.

Appendix A

SENATE BILL NO. 1074
February 10, 1911, <u>Senate Journal</u>

Introduced by Senator Finn

AN ACT

To Regulate the Ownership or Possession of Lands by Aliens.

The people of the State of California, represented by Senate and Assembly, do enact as follows:

Section 1. All aliens may, subject to the further provisions of this act, acquire and hold title in fee-simple, or otherwise, to lands, tenements and hereditaments, situate in this state, by deed, devise or descent, and may alienate, sell, assign, incumber, devise and convey lands, tenements or hereditaments whether the same have been heretofore or be hereafter acquired, and the title to any lands of which an alien may die seized or possessed, intestate, shall descend to the heirs at law, and no person shall be deprived of his right to take title to real estate as heir at law by descent from any deceased person because he may be an alien or be compelled to trace his relationship to such deceased person through one or more aliens.

Sec. 2. If any alien at the time of acquiring title to lands situate in this state shall be of the age of twenty-one years or upwards, he may hold title to the same for five years from and after the time of acquiring such title; but if any alien shall at the time of acquiring title to lands situate in this state be under the age of twenty-one years he may hold title to the same for five years after the time he becomes twenty-one years of age, and if at the end of the time above limited, such lands shall not have been conveyed to bona fide purchasers for value, or such alien shall not have become a citizen of the United States, it shall then be the duty of the district attorney of the county in which such lands are situate to proceed by information, in the name of the people of the State of California, in the superior court of such county, to compel a sale of the lands, and such court shall have jurisdiction to hear and determine such information and to order the sale of such lands by a special commissioner, or other officer, for that purpose appointed by the court, at such time and place and upon such terms as the court may direct, but such sale shall be made subject to all incumbrances by way of judgment or mortgage, or otherwise, existing against such lands. Notice to all parties interested shall be given as now authorized in civil cases.

It shall be a good defense to any such proceeding that prior to the time that the same was commenced, such alien had become a citizen of the United States, or that the title to such lands had been conveyed in good faith by such alien immediately to a citizen of the United States, or if such alien has deceased prior to the time of the commencement of such proceeding that his heirs or devisees or any person claiming by, through or under them, are or had become citizens of the United

States. Said court shall tax as costs such fees for the district attorney as shall be reasonable, not exceeding twenty per centum of the amount which shall be bid for such lands at any such sale thereof, and shall allow to such special commissioner, or other officer making such sale, the same fees as are allowed for the sale of lands under decree of foreclosure of the mortgages, and all fees and costs shall be paid out of the proceeds of sale of such real estate.

If any district attorney shall neglect or refuse to proceed by information as hereinbefore provided, within thirty days after it shall be brought to his notice that an alien is holding title to lands in this state contrary to the provisions of this act, then any citizen may proceed by information, in the name of the people of the State of California in the same manner as such district attorney might have proceeded under the provisions of this section, and he and his attorney may be allowed such reasonable fees for their services, to be taxed as costs, as the court may direct, not exceeding in the aggregate twenty per centum of the amount which shall be bid for such lands at any sale thereof. All sums received from the sale of any lands under the provisions of this act, less costs as herein provided, shall be paid to the owner, his heirs or assigns.

Sec. 3. No contract, agreement or lease of real estate for a longer period of one year shall be made to any alien, and any lease, agreement or devise of real estate made to any alien contrary to the provisions of this section shall be null and void.

Appendix B

THE ALIEN LAND LAW OF 1913 AS PROPOSED BY THE
ASIATIC EXCLUSION LEAGUE ON DECEMBER 19, 1912
Cf. A. E. L., Proceedings, pp. 278-279

AN ACT

To Regulate the Ownership and Possession of Real Property in the State of California by Certain Classes of Aliens.

The People of the State of California, represented in Senate and Assembly, do enact as follows:

Section 1. No alien who is not eligible to citizenship under the Constitution and laws of the United States of America shall acquire title to or own land or real property in the State of California, except as hereinafter provided, but he shall have and enjoy in the State of California such rights as to personal property as are or shall be accorded a citizen of the United States, under the law of the Nation to which such alien belongs, or by the treaties of such Nation with the United States, except as the same may be affected by the provisions of this Act, or the Constitution of this State.

Sec. 2. This Act shall not apply to lands or real property now owned in this State by such aliens so long as they are held by the present owners.

Sec. 3. All such aliens who may hereafter acquire real property in California by devise, descent or by purchase where such purchase is made under any legal proceedings enforcing a debt or lien in favor of such a lien, may hold the same for the period of five years and no longer from the date of so acquiring such title.

Sec. 4. Any such alien who shall hereafter hold real property in the State of California in contravention of the provisions of this Act may nevertheless convey the fee simple title thereof to any person who is legally entitled to own real property in California and to no other person at any time before the institution of escheat proceedings, as hereinafter provided; provided, however, that if any such conveyance shall be made in trust or for the purpose and with the intention of evading the provisions of this Act, such conveyance shall be null and void and the rights of all persons therein shall immediately cease and determine and any such real property so conveyed shall be forfeited and escheated to the State of California, absolutely for the benefit and use of the public-school funds.

Sec. 5. It shall be the duty of the District Attorney of the county wherein the real property is situate, or the Attorney-General of the State of California, should the District Attorney fail or neglect to act, when he shall be informed or have reason to believe that any real property in the State is being held contrary to the provisions of this Act, to institute suit in behalf of the State of California in the Superior Court of the county in which said lands are situate, praying for the escheat of the same in behalf of the State, and he shall proceed therein as in cases provided by law for escheats of lands or property where such property has no known owner; provided, that due service of process shall be made and service upon the holder of title be had as provided by law, and the court having jurisdiction shall then proceed to final judgment and the sale of the property as sales are conducted under foreclosure. It shall be a good defense to any such proceeding that the title to such lands had been prior to the commencement of such proceedings conveyed in good faith by such alien to a citizen of the United States or to an alien authorized to own real property in this State. Said court shall tax as costs such fees as shall be reasonable, not exceeding twenty per centum of the amount, which shall be bid for such lands at any such sale thereof, and shall allow to the officer making such sale the same fees as are allowed for the sale of lands under decree of foreclosure of mortgages, and all fees and costs shall be paid out of the proceeds by sale of such real estate. If any District Attorney shall neglect or refuse to proceed by information as herein provided within thirty days after it shall be brought to his notice that any such alien is holding title to lands in this State contrary to the provisions of this Act, then any citizen may proceed by information in the name of the People of the State in the same manner as such District Attorney might have proceeded under the provisions of this section, and he and his attorney may be allowed such reasonable fees for their services, to be taxed as costs, as the court may direct, not exceeding in the aggregate twenty per centum of the amount which shall be paid for such lands at the sale thereof.

Sec. 6. In case the lands at the time escheat proceedings are about to be commenced are owned by a minor or minors or by a person or persons of unsound mind the process herein provided shall be served as provided by law upon the guardian of the minor or minors or person or persons of unsound mind, and if there is no such guardian the District Attorney or the Attorney-General of the State shall make application in the name of the People of the State to the court having jurisdiction and procure the appointment of a guardian ad litem, to represent such minor or minors or person or persons of unsound mind in such proceedings, and such guardian or guardians ad litem shall appear and defend the action.

Sec. 7. If it shall be determined upon the trial of any such proceedings that lands are held contrary to the provisions of this Act, the court trying such cause shall render judgment condemning such lands and ordering the same to be sold under an order of the court as in cases of sale under foreclosure proceedings; the proceeds of such sale after deducting the costs of the proceeding shall be paid to the clerk of the court rendering the judgment, where the same shall remain for one year from the date of such payment, subject to the order of the alien owner of such lands, his heirs and legal representatives, and if not claimed within the period of one year such clerk shall pay the same into the treasury of the State for the benefit of the available school funds of the State; provided, that when any money shall have been paid to the State Treasurer as herein provided the alien or his heirs may procure the same to be returned by applying for and procuring an order from the court condemning the property showing that such judgment escheating such property was procured by fraud or mistake, or that there was material irregularity in the proceedings; this application, however, must be made within two years from the date such moneys were turned over to the State Treasury; provided, further, that in no event shall the State be liable or called upon to refund any further sum than the actual cash transmitted and delivered to such treasury.

Sec. 8. Every contract agreement or lease of any land made with or to any alien not eligible to citizenship under the laws of the United States shall be null and void.

Appendix C

ALIEN LAND LAW OF 1913, STATUTES OF CALIFORNIA,
1913, Chapter 113, pp. 206-208

Section 1. All aliens eligible to citizenship under the laws of the United States may acquire, possess, enjoy, transmit and inherit real property, or any interest therein, in this state, in the same manner and to the same extent as citizens of the United States, except as otherwise provided by the laws of this state.

Sec. 2. All aliens other than those mentioned in section one of this act may acquire, possess, enjoy and transfer real property, or any interest therein, in this state, in the manner and to the extent and for the purposes prescribed by any treaty now existing between the government of the United States and the nation or country of which such alien is a citizen or subject, and not otherwise, and may in addition thereto lease lands in this state for agricultural purposes for a term not exceeding three years.

Sec. 3. Any company, association or corporation organized under the laws of this or any other state or nation, of which a majority of the members are aliens other than those specified in section one of this act, or in which a majority of the issued capital stock is owned by such aliens, may acquire, possess, enjoy and convey real property, or any interest therein, in this state, in the manner and to the extent and for the purposes prescribed by any treaty now existing between the government of the United States and the nation or country of which such members or stockholders are citizens or subjects, and not otherwise, and may in addition thereto lease lands in this state for agricultural purposes for a term not exceeding three years.

Sec. 4. Whenever it appears to the court in any probate proceeding that by reason of the provisions of this act any heir or devisee can not take real property in this state which, but for said provisions, said heir or devisee would take as such, the court, instead of ordering a distribution of such real property to such heir or devisee, shall order a sale of said real property to be made in the manner provided by law for probate sales of real property, and the proceeds of such sale shall be distributed to such heir or devisee in lieu of such real property.

Sec. 5. Any real property hereafter acquired in fee in violation of the provisions of this act by any alien mentioned in section two of this act, or by any company, association or corporation mentioned in section three of this act, shall escheat to, and become and remain the property of the State of California. The attorney general shall institute proceedings to have the escheat of such real property adjudged and enforced in the manner provided by section 474 of the Political Code and title eight, part three of the Code of Civil Procedure. Upon the entry of final judgment in such proceedings, the title to such real property shall pass to the State of California. The provisions of this section and of sections two and three of this act shall not apply to any real property hereafter acquired in the enforcement or in satisfaction of any lien now existing upon, or interest in such property, so long as such real property so acquired shall remain the property of the alien, company, association or corporation acquiring the same in such manner.

Sec. 6. Any leasehold or other interest in real property less than the fee, hereafter acquired in violation of the provisions of this act by any alien mentioned in section two of this act, or by any company, association or corporation mentioned in section three of this act, shall escheat to the State of California. The attorney general shall institute proceedings to have such escheat adjudged and enforced as provided in section five of this act. In such proceedings the court shall determine and adjudge the value of such leasehold, or other interest in such real property, and enter judgment for the state for the amount thereof together with costs. Thereupon the court shall order a sale of the real property covered by such leasehold, or other interest, in the manner provided by section 1271 of the Code of Civil Procedure. Out of the proceeds arising from such sale, the amount of the judgment rendered for the state shall be paid into the state treasury and the balance shall be deposited with and distributed by the court in accordance with the interest of the parties therein.

Sec. 7. Nothing in this act shall be construed as a limitation upon the power of the state to enact laws with respect to the acquisition, holding or disposal by aliens of real property in this state.

Sec. 8. All acts and parts of acts inconsistent, or in conflict with the provisions of this act, are hereby repealed.

Appendix D

PROPOSITION NUMBER ONE, ADOPTED NOVEMBER 2, 1920,
STATUTES OF CALIFORNIA, 1921, pp. lxxxiii-lxxxvi

The people of the State of California do enact as follows:

Section 1. All aliens eligible to citizenship under the laws of the United States may acquire, possess, enjoy, transmit and inherit real property, or any interest therein, in this state, in the same manner and to the same extent as citizens of the United States, except as otherwise provided by the laws of this state.

Sec. 2. All aliens other than those mentioned in section one of this act may acquire, possess, enjoy and transfer real property, or any interest therein, in this state, in the manner and to the extent and for the purpose prescribed by any treaty now existing between the government of the United States and the nation or country of which such alien is a citizen or subject, and not otherwise.

Sec. 3. Any company, association or corporation organized under the laws of this or any other state or nation, of which a majority of the members are aliens other than those specified in section one of this act, or in which a majority of the issued capital stock is owned by such aliens, may acquire, possess, enjoy and convey real property, or any interest therein, in this state, in the manner and to the extent and for the purposes prescribed by any treaty now existing between the government of the United States and the nation or country of which such members or stockholders are citizens or subjects, and not otherwise. Hereafter all aliens other than those specified in section one hereof may become members of or acquire shares of stock in any company, association or corporation that is or may be authorized to acquire, possess, enjoy or convey agricultural land, in the manner and to the extent and for the purposes prescribed by any treaty now existing between the government of the United States and the nation or country of which such alien is a citizen or subject, and not otherwise.

Sec. 4. Hereafter no alien mentioned in section two hereof and no company, association or corporation mentioned in section three hereof, may be appointed guardian of that portion of the estate of a minor which consists of property which such alien or such company, association or corporation is inhibited from acquiring, possessing, enjoying or transferring by reason of the provisions of this act. The public administrator of the proper county, or any other competent person or corporation, may be appointed guardian of the estate of a minor citizen whose parents are ineligible to appointment under the provisions of this section.

On such notice to the guardian as the court may require, the superior court may remove the guardian of such an estate whenever it appears to the satisfaction of the court:
    (a) That the guardian has failed to file the report required by the provisions of section five hereof; or
    (b) That the property of the ward has not been or is not being administered with due regard to the primary interest of the ward; or

(c) That facts exist which would make the guardian ineligible to appointment in the first instance; or
(d) That facts establishing any other legal ground for removal exist.

Sec. 5. (a) The term "trustee" as used in this section means any person, company, association or corporation that as guardian, trustee, attorney-in-fact or agent, or in any other capacity has the title, custody or control of property, or some interest therein, belonging to an alien mentioned in section two hereof, or to the minor child of such an alien, if the property is of such a character that such alien is inhibited from acquiring, possessing, enjoying or transferring it.

(b) Annually on or before the thirty-first day of January every such trustee must file in the office of the Secretary of State of California and in the office of the county clerk of each county in which any of the property is situated, a verified written report showing:

(1) The property, real or personal, held by him for or on behalf of such alien or minor;

(2) A statement showing the date when each item of such property came into his possession or control;

(3) An itemized account of all expenditures, investments, rents, issues and profits in respect to the administration and control of such property with particular reference to holdings of corporate stock and leases, cropping contracts and other agreements in respect to land and the handling or sale of products thereof.

(c) Any person, company, association or corporation that violates any provision of this section is guilty of a misdemeanor and shall be punished by a fine not exceeding one thousand dollars or by imprisonment in the county jail not exceeding one year, or by both such fine and imprisonment.

(d) The provisions of this section are cumulative and are not intended to change the jurisdiction or the rules of practice of courts of justice.

Sec. 6. Whenever it appears to the court in any probate proceeding that by reason of the provisions of this act any heir or devisee cannot take real property in this state or membership or shares of stock in a company, association or corporation which, but for said provisions, said heir or devisee would take as such, the court, instead of ordering a distribution of such property to such heir or devisee, shall order a sale of said property to be made in the manner provided by law for probate sales of property and the proceeds of such sale shall be distributed to such heir or devisee in lieu of such property.

Sec. 7. Any real property hereafter acquired in fee in violation of the provisions of this act by any alien mentioned in section two of this act, or by any company, association or corporation mentioned in section three of this act, shall escheat to, and become and remain the property of the State of California. The Attorney General or district attorney of the proper county shall institute proceedings to have the escheat of such real property adjudged and enforced in the manner provided by section four hundred seventy-four of the Political Code and title eight, part three of the Code of Civil Procedure. Upon the entry of final judgment in such proceedings, the title to such real property shall pass to the State of California. The provisions of this section and of sections two and three of this act shall not apply to any real property hereafter acquired in the enforcement or in satisfaction of any lien now existing upon, or interest in such property, so long as such real property so acquired shall remain the property of the alien, company, association or corporation acquiring the same in such manner. No alien, company, association or corporation mentioned in section two or section three hereof shall hold for a longer period than two years the possession of any agricultural land acquired in the enforcement of or in satisfaction of a mortgage or other lien hereafter made or acquired in good faith to secure a debt.

Sec. 8. Any leasehold or other interest in real property less than the fee, hereafter acquired in violation of the provisions of this act by any alien mentioned in section two of this act, or by any company, association or corporation mentioned in section three of this act, shall escheat to the State of California. The Attorney General or district attorney of the proper county shall institute proceedings to have such escheat adjudged and enforced as provided in section seven of this act. In such proceedings the court shall determine and adjudge the value of such leasehold or other interest in such real property, and enter judgment for the state for the amount thereof together with costs. Thereupon the court shall order a sale of the real property covered by such leasehold, or other interest, in the manner provided by section twelve hundred seventy-one of the Code of Civil Procedure. Out of the proceeds arising from such sale, the amount of the judgment rendered for the state shall be paid into the state treasury and the balance shall be deposited with and distributed by the court in accordance with interest of the parties therein. Any share of stock or the interest of any member in a company, association or corporation hereafter acquired in violation of the provisions of section three of this act shall escheat to the State of California. Such escheat shall be adjudged and enforced in the same manner as provided in this section for the escheat of a leasehold or other interest in real property less than the fee.

Sec. 9. Every transfer of real property, or of an interest therein, though colorable in form, shall be void as to the state and the interest thereby conveyed or sought to be conveyed shall escheat to the state if the property interest involved is of such a character that an alien mentioned in section two hereof is inhibited from acquiring, possessing, enjoying or transferring it, and if the conveyance is made with intent to prevent, evade or avoid escheat as provided for herein.

A prima facie presumption that the conveyance is made with such intent shall arise upon proof of any of the following groups of facts:

(a) The taking of the property in the name of a person other than the persons mentioned in section two hereof if the consideration is paid or agreed or understood to be paid by an alien mentioned in section two hereof;
(b) The taking of the property in the name of a company, association or corporation, if the memberships or shares of stock therein held by aliens mentioned in section two hereof, together with the memberships or shares of stock held by others but paid for or agreed or understood to be paid for by such aliens, would amount to a majority of the membership or the issued capital stock of such company, association or corporation;
(c) The execution of a mortgage in favor of an alien mentioned in section two hereof if said mortgage is given possession, control or management of the property.

The enumeration in this section of certain presumptions shall not be so construed as to preclude other presumptions or inferences that reasonably may be made as to the existence of intent to prevent, evade or avoid escheat as provided for herein.

Sec. 10. If two or more persons conspire to effect a transfer of real property, or of an interest therein, in violation of the provisions hereof, they are punishable by imprisonment in the county jail or state penitentiary not exceeding two years, or by a fine not exceeding five thousand dollars, or both.

Sec. 11. Nothing in this act shall be construed as a limitation upon the power of the state to enact laws with respect to the acquisition, holding or disposal by aliens of real property in this state.

Sec. 12. All acts and parts of acts inconsistent or in conflict with the provisions hereof are hereby repealed; provided, that--

(a) This act shall not affect pending actions or proceedings, but the same may be prosecuted and defended with the same effect as if this act had not been adopted;
(b) No cause of action arising under any law of this state shall be affected by reason of the adoption of this act whether an action or proceeding has been instituted thereon at the time of the taking effect of this act or not and actions may be brought upon such causes in the same manner, under the same terms and conditions, and with the same effect as if this act had not been adopted;
(c) This act in so far as it does not add to, take from or alter an existing law, shall be construed as a continuation thereof.

Sec. 13. The legislature may amend this act in furtherance of its purpose and to facilitate its operation.

Sec. 14. If any section, subsection, sentence, clause or phrase of this act is for any reason held to be unconstitutional, such decision shall not affect the validity of the remaining portions of this act. The people hereby declare that they would have passed this act, and each section, subsection, sentence, clause and phrase thereof, irrespective of the fact that any one or more other sections, subsections, sentences, clauses or phrases be declared unconstitutional.

Appendix E

ALIEN LAND LAW OF 1923, STATUTES OF CALIFORNIA, 1923,
Chapter 441, pp. 1,020-1,025

Section 1. Section one of an act entitled "An act relating to the rights, powers and disabilities of aliens and of certain companies, associations and corporations with respect to property in this state, providing for escheats in certain cases, prescribing the procedure therein, requiring reports of certain property holdings to facilitate the enforcement of this act, prescribing penalties for violation of the provisions hereof, and repealing all acts or parts of acts inconsistent or in conflict herewith," adopted and approved by the electors of the State of California, November 2, 1920, is hereby amended to read as follows:

Section 1. All aliens eligible to citizenship under the laws of the United States may acquire, possess, enjoy, use, cultivate, occupy, transfer, transmit and inherit real property, or any interest therein, in this state, and have in whole or in part the beneficial use thereof, in the same manner and to the same extent as citizens of the United States, except as otherwise provided by the laws of this state.

Sec. 2. Section two of said act is hereby amended to read as follows:

Sec. 2. All aliens other than those mentioned in section one of this act may acquire, possess, enjoy, use, cultivate, occupy and transfer real property, or any interest therein, in this state, and have in whole or in part the beneficial use thereof, in the manner and to the extent, and for the purposes prescribed by any treaty now existing between the government of the United States and the nation or country of which such alien is a citizen or subject, and not otherwise.

Sec. 3. Section three of said act is hereby amended to read as follows:

Sec. 3. Any company, association or corporation organized under the laws of this or any other state or nation, of which a majority of the members are aliens other than those specified in section one of this act, or in which a majority of the issued capital stock is owned by such aliens, may acquire, possess, enjoy, use, cultivate, occupy and transfer real property, or any interest therein, in this state, and have in whole or in part the beneficial use thereof, in the manner and to the extent and for the purposes prescribed by any treaty now existing between the government of the United States and the nation or country of which such members or stockholders are citizens or subjects, and not otherwise. Hereafter all aliens other than those specified in section one hereof may become members of or acquire shares of stock in any company, association or corporation that is or may be authorized to acquire, possess, enjoy, use, cultivate, occupy and transfer real property, or any interest therein, in this state, in the manner and to the extent and for the purposes prescribed by any treaty now existing between the government of the United States and the nation or country of which such alien is a citizen or subject, and not otherwise.

Sec. 4. Section four of said act is hereby amended to read as follows:

Sec. 4. Hereafter no alien mentioned in section two hereof and no company, association or corporation mentioned in section three hereof, may be appointed guardian of that portion of the estate of a minor which consists of property which such alien is inhibited from acquiring, possessing, enjoying, using, cultivating, occupying, transferring, transmitting or inheriting, or which such company, association or corporation is inhibited from acquiring, possessing, enjoying, using, cultivating, occupying or transferring, by reason of the provisions of this act. The public administrator of the proper county, or any other competent person or corporation, may be appointed guardian of the estate of a minor citizen whose parents are ineligible to appointment under the provisions of this section.

On such notice to the guardian as the court may require, the superior court may remove the guardian of such an estate whenever it appears to the satisfaction of the court:

(a) That the guardian has failed to file the report required by the provisions of section five hereof; or
(b) That the property of the ward has not been or is not being administered with due regard to the primary interest of the ward; or
(c) That facts exist which would make the guardian ineligible to appointment in the first instance; or
(d) That facts establishing any other legal ground for removal exist.

Sec. 5. Section five of said act is hereby amended to read as follows:

Sec. 5. (a) The term "trustee" as used in this section means any person, company, association or corporation that as guardian, trustee, attorney in fact or agent, or in any other capacity has the title, custody or control of property, or some interest therein, belonging to an alien mentioned in section two hereof, or to the minor child of such an alien, if the property is of such a character that such alien is inhibited from acquiring, possessing, enjoying, using, cultivating, occupying, transferring, transmitting or inheriting it.

(b) Annually on or before the thirty-first day of January every such trustee must file in the office of the secretary of state of California and in the office of the county clerk of each county in which any of the property is situated, a verified written report showing:

(1) The property, real or personal, held by him for or on behalf of such alien or minor;
(2) A statement showing the date when each item of such property came into his possession or control;
(3) An itemized account of all such expenditures, investments, rents, issues and profits in respect to the administration and control of such property with particular reference to holdings of corporate stock and leases, cropping contracts and other agreements in respect to land and the handling or sale of products thereof.

(c) Any person, company, association or corporation that violates any provision of this section is guilty of a misdemeanor and shall be punished by a fine not exceeding one thousand dollars or by imprisonment in the county jail not exceeding one year, or by both such fine and imprisonment.

(d) The provisions of this section are cumulative and are not intended to change the jurisdiction or the rules of practice of courts of justice.

Sec. 6. Section seven of said act is hereby amended to read as follows:

Sec. 7. Any real property hereafter acquired in fee in violation of the provisions of this act by any alien mentioned in section two of this act, or by any company, association or corporation mentioned in section three of this act, shall escheat as of the date of such acquiring to, and become and remain the property of the State of California. The attorney general or district attorney of the proper county shall institute proceedings to have the escheat of such real property adjudged and enforced in the manner provided by section four hundred seventy-four of the Political Code and title eight, part three of the Code of Civil Procedure. Upon the entry of final judgment in such proceedings, the title to such real property shall pass to the State of California, as of the date of such acquisition in violation of the provisions of this act. The provisions of this section and of sections two and three of this act shall not apply to any real property hereafter acquired in the enforcement or in satisfaction of any lien now existing upon or interest in such property so long as such real property so acquired shall remain the property of the alien, company, association or corporation acquiring the same in such manner. No alien, company, association or corporation mentioned in section two or section three hereof shall hold for a longer period than two years the possession of any agricultural land acquired in the enforcement of or in satisfaction of a mortgage or other lien hereafter made or acquired in good faith to secure a debt.

Sec. 7. Section eight of said act is hereby amended to read as follows:

Sec. 8. Any leasehold or other interest in real property less than the fee, including cropping contracts which are hereby declared to constitute an interest in real property less than the fee, hereafter acquired in violation of the provisions of this act by any alien mentioned in section two of this act, or by any company, association or corporation mentioned in section three of this act, shall escheat to the State of California, as of the date of such acquiring in violation of the provisions of this act. The attorney general or district attorney of the proper county shall institute proceedings to have such escheat adjudged and enforced in the same manner as is provided in section seven of this act. In such proceedings the court shall determine and adjudge the value of such leasehold or other interest in such real property, as of the date of such acquisition in violation of the provisions of this act, and enter judgment for the state for the amount thereof together with costs. The said judgment so entered shall be considered a lien against the real property in which such leasehold or other interest less than the fee is so acquired in violation of the provisions of this act, which lien shall exist as of the date of such unlawful acquisition. Thereupon the court shall order a sale of the real property covered by such leasehold, or other interest, in the manner provided by section one thousand two hundred seventy-one of the Code of Civil Procedure. Out of the proceeds arising from such sale, the amount of the judgment rendered for the state shall be paid into the state treasury and the balance shall be deposited with and distributed by the court in accordance with the interest of the parties therein. Any share of stock or the interest of any member in a company, association or corporation hereafter acquired in violation of the provisions of section three of this act shall escheat to the State of California as of the date of such acquiring in violation of the provisions of said section three of this act, and it is hereby declared that any such share of stock or the interest of any member in such a company, association or corporation so acquired in violation of the provisions of section three of this act is an interest in real property. Such escheat shall be adjudged and enforced in the same manner as is provided in this section for the escheat of a leasehold or other interest in real property less than the fee.

Sec. 8. Section nine of said act is hereby amended to read as follows:

Sec. 9. Every transfer of real property, or of an interest therein, though colorable in form, shall be void as to the state and the interest thereby conveyed or sought to be conveyed shall escheat to the state as of the date of such transfer, if the property interest involved is of such a character that an alien mentioned in section two hereof is inhibited from acquiring, possessing, enjoying, using, cultivating, occupying, transferring, transmitting or inheriting it, and if the conveyance is made with intent to prevent, evade or avoid escheat as provided for herein.

A prima facie presumption that the conveyance is made with such intent shall arise upon proof of any of the following groups of facts:

(a) The taking of the property in the name of a person other than the persons mentioned in section two hereof if the consideration is paid or agreed or understood to be paid by an alien mentioned in section two hereof;

(b) The taking of the property in the name of a company, association or corporation if the memberships or shares of stock therein held by aliens mentioned in section two hereof, together with the memberships or shares of stock held by others but paid for or agreed or understood to be paid for by such aliens, would amount to a majority of the membership or issued capital stock of such company, association or corporation;

(c) The execution of a mortgage in favor of an alien mentioned in section two hereof if such mortgagee is given possession, control or management of the property.

The enumeration in this section of certain presumptions shall not be so construed as to preclude other presumptions or inferences that reasonably may be made as to the existence of intent to prevent, evade or avoid escheat as provided for herein.

Sec. 9. Section ten of said act is hereby amended to read as follows:

Sec. 10. If two or more persons conspire to violate any of the provisions of this act they are punishable by imprisonment in the county jail or state penitentiary not exceeding two years or by a fine not exceeding five thousand dollars, or both.

Sec. 10. Section eleven of said act is hereby amended to read as follows:

Sec. 11. Nothing in this act shall be construed as a limitation upon the power of the state to enact laws with respect to the acquisition, possession, enjoyment, use, cultivation, occupation, transferring, transmitting or inheriting by aliens of real property in this state.

BIBLIOGRAPHY

Manuscripts

Bradford, Hugh, Scrapbook pertaining to the Alien Land Law of 1913. California State Library, Sacramento.

Budd, James H., MSS, Governor's Papers, GP6:117-121, California State Archives, Sacramento.

Gillett, James N., MSS, Governor's Papers, GP7:83-103, California State Archives, Sacramento.

Theses and Dissertations

Gothberg, John A., The Japanese in California and the 1920 Fight for Land Rights, Masters Thesis, Stanford University, California, 1950.

Kessler, James B., The Political Factors in California's Anti-Alien Land Legislation, 1912-1913, Doctoral Dissertation, Stanford University, California, 1958.

Matson, Floyd W., The Anti Japanese Movement in California, 1890-1942, Masters Thesis, University of California, Berkeley, 1953.

Rowell, Edward J., The Union Labor Party of San Francisco, 1901-1911, Doctoral Dissertation, University of California, Berkeley, 1938.

State and Federal Government Publications

California. Appendix to the Journal of the Senate and Assembly of the Fortieth Session of the State of California, III, 1913.

_____. Bureau of Labor Statistics. Seventh Biennial Report of the Bureau of Labor Statistics, 1895-96, Sacramento, 1896.

_____. _____. Ninth Biennial Report of the Bureau of Labor Statistics, 1899-1900, Sacramento, 1900.

_____. _____. Tenth Biennial Report of the Bureau of Labor Statistics, 1901-1902, Sacramento, 1902.

_____. _____. Fourteenth Biennial Report of the Bureau of Labor Statistics, 1909-1910, Sacramento, 1910.

California. Governor's Biennial Messages, 1905-1925.

_____. Journal of the Assembly During the Thirty-Ninth Session of the Legislature of the State of California, 1911.

_____. Journal of the Senate During the Thirty-Eighth Session of the Legislature of the State of California, 1909.

_____. Journal of the Senate During the Fortieth Session of the Legislature of the State of California, 1913.

_____. Secretary of State. Statement of the Vote at the General Election held on November 8, 1910.

_____. _____. Statement of the Vote at the General Election held on November 5, 1946.

_____. _____. Statement of the Vote at the General Election held on November 6, 1956.

_____. State Board of Control. California and the Oriental, State Printing Office, Sacramento, 1922.

_____. Statutes of California and Amendments to the Constitution Passed at the Thirty-Eighth Session of the Legislature, 1909.

_____. Statutes of California and Amendments to the Codes Passed at the Fortieth Session of the Legislature, 1913.

United States. Department of Labor. Bureau of Immigration. Annual Report of the Commissioner General of Immigration to the Secretary of Labor, Washington, June 1915.

_____. _____. _____. Annual Report of the Commissioner General of Immigration to the Secretary of Labor, Washington, June 1920.

_____. House of Representatives. Committee on Immigration and Naturalization. Hearings on Japanese Immigration, parts 1-4, Washington, 1921.

_____. Senate. Committee on Immigration. Japanese Immigration Legislation: Hearings on S. 2576, March 11-13; 15, 1924, 68th Congress, First Session, Washington, 1924.

Newspapers

Los Angeles Evening Herald

Oakland Enquirer

Sacramento Bee

Sacramento Record Union

San Francisco Argonaut

San Francisco Call

San Francisco Chronicle

San Francisco Evening Bulletin

San Francisco Examiner

Books

Adamic, Louis, Dynamite; the Story of Class Violence in America, New York, Viking Press, 1934.

Bailey, Thomas A., Theodore Roosevelt and the Japanese-American Crisis, California, Stanford University Press, 1934.

Beach, Walter G., Oriental Crime in California, California, Stanford University Press, 1932.

Bean, Walton, California, An Interpretive History, New York, McGraw-Hill Co., 1968.

Coletta, Paolo E., William Jennings Bryan, II. Progressive Politician and Moral Statesman, 1909-1915, Lincoln, University of Nebraska Press, 1969.

Coolidge, Mary R., Chinese Immigration, New York, Henry Holt Co., 1909.

Cross, Ira B., A History of the Labor Movement in California, California, University of California Press, Berkeley, 1935.

Daniels, Roger, The Politics of Prejudice: The Anti-Japanese Movement in California and the Struggle for Japanese Exclusion, California, University of California Press, Berkeley and Los Angeles, 1962.

Dillon, Richard H., Shanghaiing Days, New York, Coward-McConn, Inc., 1961.

Esthus, Raymond A., Theodore Roosevelt and Japan, Seattle and London, University of Washington Press, 1966.

Gompers, Samuel, Seventy Years of Life and Labor, New York, E. P. Dutton and Co., 1948.

Gulick, Sidney L., The American-Japanese Problem; a Study of the Racial Relations of the East and West, New York, Charles Scribner's Sons, 1914.

Hichborn, Franklin, Story of the Session of the California Legislature of 1909, San Francisco, James H. Barry Co., 1909.

_____, Story of the Session of the California Legislature of 1911, San Francisco, James H. Barry Co., 1911.

Hichborn, Franklin, <u>Story of the Session of the California Legislature of 1913</u>, San Francisco, James H. Barry Co., 1913.

_____, <u>Story of the Session of the California Legislature of 1915</u>, San Francisco, James H. Barry Co., 1916.

Higham, John, <u>Strangers in the Land; Patterns of American Nativism, 1860-1925</u>, New Jersey, Rutgers University Press, 1955.

Hunt, Rockwell D., <u>California's Stately Hall of Fame</u>, 1950.

Ichihashi, Yamato, <u>Japanese in the United States: A Critical Study of the Problems of the Japanese Immigrants and Their Children</u>, California, Stanford University Press, 1932.

Kawakami, K. K., <u>The Real Japanese Question</u>, New York, Macmillan Co., 1921.

Mears, Elliot G., <u>Resident Orientals on the American Pacific Coast: Their Legal and Economic Status</u>, Chicago, University of Chicago Press, 1928.

Millis, H. A., <u>The Japanese Problem in the United States</u>, New York, Macmillan Co., 1915.

Olin, Spencer C., Jr., <u>California's Prodigal Sons: Hiram Johnson and the Progressives, 1911-1917</u>, California, University of California Press, Berkeley and Los Angeles, 1968.

Ryan, Frederick L., <u>Industrial Relations in the San Francisco Building Trades</u>, Norman, University of Oklahoma Press, 1935.

Steffens, Lincoln, <u>The Autobiography of Lincoln Steffens</u>, New York, Harcourt, Brace, 1931.

tenBroek, Jacobus, Edward N. Barnhart and Floyd W. Matson, <u>Prejudice, War and the Constitution: Causes and Consequences of the Evacuation of the Japanese-Americans in World War II</u>, California, University of California Press, Berkeley and Los Angeles, 1968.

Trevor, John B., <u>Japanese Exclusion, A Study of the Policy and the Law</u>, U.S., 68th Congress, 2nd Session, House Document 600, Washington, 1925.

<u>West's Annotated California Codes</u>, St. Paul, 1954.

Pamphlets

American Committee of Justice, <u>California and the Japanese, a Compilation of Arguments Advertised in Newspapers by the American Committee of Justice in Opposition to the Alien Land Law, Together With the Memorial Addressed to Congress by the Said Committee</u>, Oakland, California, The American Committee of Justice, 1920.

Asiatic Exclusion League, Pacific Coast Convention of the Anti-Jap Laundry League, San Francisco, May 9, 1909, in Japanese Pamphlets, I, California Room, California State Library, Sacramento.

_____, Proceedings of the Asiatic Exclusion League, San Francisco, December 1907--March 1913.

_____, Proceedings of the First International Convention of the Asiatic Exclusion League of North America, Seattle, Washington, February 3-5, 1908.

Chinese Pamphlets, California Room, California State Library, Sacramento.

Magazine Articles

Abbott, Lyman, "The Alien Land Bill in California," The Outlook, 104 (April 19, 1913), pp. 828-829.

_____, "The Japanese in California: A Poll of the Press," The Outlook, 104 (May 3, 1913), pp. 22-24.

Buell, Raymond L., "The Development of the Anti-Japanese Agitation in the United States, I," Political Science Quarterly, 37 (1922), pp. 605-638.

_____, "The Development of the Anti-Japanese Agitation in the United States, II," Political Science Quarterly, 38 (1923), pp. 57-81.

Coletta, Paolo E., "The Most Thankless Task: Bryan and the California Alien Land Legislation," Pacific Historical Review, 36 (May 1967), pp. 163-187.

Edwards, Percy L., "The Industrial Side of the Alien Land Law Problem," Overland Monthly, 62 (August 1913), pp. 190-200.

Grivas, Theodore, "A History of the Los Angeles Young Men's Christian Association: The First Twenty Years," California Historical Society Quarterly, 44 (September 1965), pp. 205-227.

Hennings, Robert E., "James D. Phelan and the Woodrow Wilson Anti-Oriental Statement of May 3, 1912," California Historical Society Quarterly, 42 (December 1963), pp. 291-300.

Inman, J. M., "The Time Has Arrived to Eliminate the Japs as California Landholders," Grizzly Bear, 37 (June 1920), pp. 4-5.

Millis, H. A., "California and the Japanese," The Survey, 30 (June 1913), pp. 332-336.

Penrose, Eldon R., "Grape Juice Diplomacy and a Bit of Political Buncombe," Pacific Historical Review, 37 (May 1968), pp. 159-162.

Phelan, James D., "The Japanese Question from a Californian's Standpoint," The Independent, 74 (June 26, 1913), pp. 1,439-1,440.

Yoell, A. E., "Oriental vs. American Labor," *The Annals of the American Academy of Social and Political Sciences*, 34 (September 1909), pp. 247-256.

Bibliographies

California State Library. "Alien Ownership of Land," *News Notes of California Libraries*, 9 (1914), pp. 683-86.

Hennefound, Helen E. and Orpha Cummings (Comp)., *Bibliography of the Japanese in American Agriculture*, Washington, United States Department of Agriculture, Bibliographical Bulletin #3, 1943.

Johnson, Julia E., *Japanese Exclusion*, New York, H. W. Wilson Co., 1925.

Jones, Helen D., *Japanese in the United States*, Washington, Library of Congress General Reference and Bibliography Division, 1946. (Mimeographed.)

Printed in Taiwan